NEW PLAINS REVIEW

FALL 2011

Executive Editor
Shay Rahm-Barnett

Editor-in-Chief
James C. Gibbs

Nonfiction Editor
Jesse Peters

Poetry Editor
Evelyn Dayringer

Assistant Poetry Editor
Caroline Verdea

Fiction Editor
Kellea Ingram

Assistant Editor
Makia Turner

Editor-in-Chief
ScissorTale Review
Kellea Ingram

Associate Editor
ScissorTale Review
Caroline Verdea

Production Chief
Michelle Waggoner

Web Consultant
William Andrews

Cover Art
Sandy Sandy

Section Photography
David Parks

New Plains Review, Volume 12, Number 1
$10.00

Back issues available through the *New Plains Review* office.

New Plains Review is a literary journal published each academic semester, sponsored by the English Department, College of Liberal Arts, the University of Central Oklahoma.

New Plains Review accepts original work in prose, poetry, drama, fiction, art, and photography. Typed submissions are accepted by email.

Email submissions: newplainsreview@gmail.com
Website: http://www.libarts.uco.edu/english/newplains

New Plains Review
100 North University Drive
Edmond, Oklahoma 73034
Phone: (405) 974-5613

The logo image found on every cover of *New Plains* since 2000 is based on a painting titled "Phantom Warriors" by acclaimed Native American artist and UCO alumnus Sherman Chaddlesone.

Affirmative Action and ADA Statement:

In compliance with Title VI of the Civil Rights Act of 1964, Executive Order 11246 as amended. Title IX of the Education Amendments of 1972. Sections 503 and 504 of the Rehabilitation Act of 1973 and other Federal Laws and Regulations. UCO does not discriminate on the basis of race, color, national origin, sex, age, religion, handicap, disability, or status as a veteran in any of its policies, practices, or procedures; this includes but is not limited to admissions, employment, financial aid, and educational services.

FOREWORD

"So, please, oh please, we beg, we pray, go throw your TV set away,
and in its place you can install, a lovely bookcase on the wall."
– Roald Dahl

I am pleased to present to you, on behalf of the English Department,
College of Liberal Arts, University of Central Oklahoma, the Fall
2011 edition of the *New Plains Review*.

Shay Rahm-Barnett, Executive Editor
October 2011

New Plains Review is published semiannually in the spring and fall
by the University of Central Oklahoma and is staffed by faculty
and students. We are committed to publishing high quality poetry,
fiction and creative non-fiction by established and emerging writers.

CONTENTS

FICTION

NONFICTION

ABOUT THE AUTHORS

POETRY

James Welsh

Benediction for the Outside

I trust these hands shall never rust
through a flurry of April dust. As
an obscure writing hand once said,
April is indeed the cruelest month,
sadistic with its teeth, waking the
world up from a slumber numbered
in dreams—the only way we
should count things. Our hearts
once murmured that count without
a murmur to its beats.

I trust we will march through the
April, that we will still be those thumps
knocking into the dawn for summer.

I trust there will be big fish in the pond—
I've been meaning to learn how to walk
for ages. I trust that since the weak
learn to speak with kick and fist,
I will learn to talk.

I trust I'll never be what I saw in the morning mirror.
I can never be the push against my pull—
the timid madness would rip me down
the center—antiseptic clean—an equator
pulled out of shape by the poles.
And I trust these watches, these clocks,
these seasons, these calendars, these
times will change as long as we can
change them at the registers.

Aw-o-tan Nisgah

beneath

for Homero Aridjis

thirsty for dust, the earth grovels at your feet
like a blind street beggar who's never known the indignity
of alcohol, overpasses, generosity, dirt

"spare a body?" it asks so simply, so softly,
so sweetly, like a puma lapping nectar from its paw,
you'd think it was that solitary cloud hovering overhead
calling down to you and not this dull expanse extending
unobstructed to the horizon, lazy beneath a sky
that, at least, had the initiative to ponder up this single cloud

and if the sky can offer one wispy cloud, surely you can offer one
body—your body, yes, but nothing so valuable as your soul,
which you've already auctioned off anyways; and as you ponder
your decision, you begin to weigh the necessity of your body,
that perhaps you'd be better off without it, burdensome as it is,
an asymmetrical mass of flesh and bone, a cadaverous corpse,
a corpse, a corpse after all—and how unexquisite in contrast
to your soul, which knows as if by heart the emotions
of minerals, languages of leaves, the names the rainbows call
themselves at the points where they touch the earth
and where these sacred sites hide and how the earth feels there
and there, caressed by their colors, most of which you'll never see

nor have you ever seen your soul, and with that sold off,
you never will—but you've seen this body, your body, as you say,
and the earth has seen neither, will never see, blind as it is from
    seeing
so much, too much, too many, so that it can only guess by the
    feeling
of your monotonous trudging over its face that this body, your
    body,
must rise to something—grace, or something like it—and so
must have a drop to share, if not all, at the end of it, at the end
of the earth, somewhere so far beyond that it is here right now
                                  beneath you

Daniel Saunders

Do Not Be Confused,
For Seek And Ye Shall Find

What are we but the shapeless shifters of the shapeless
    shifting night.
We are the vagrants vaguely gallivanting about the broken
    yards measuring by yards
How far we've come in this moonlight, the fantastical lift of
    our spirits
By restless spirits no one sees but can be seen in the deepest
    blackness
Of a moonless night we have yet to see but be seen by
    watchful eyes.
It is not hope that drives us to our doomed fate but a fatal
    drifting
To sleep with no rest but a rest stop ahead for this our
    speeding soul.
Drink to our health and drink to our death but do not drink
    to death our health.
Meaning found in this mean spirited quest to find the means
    to spirit us away
And we have found it, but not where we looked, for we
    looked to those leading us
With lead soles dragging down their souls and us with them.
It is our own fault they are not to seek blame, blame not
    them but ourselves.
Fifteen cents in a holey pocket, a holy book, and a wholly
    found sense of adventure.
Where to go from here but down, down to our fatal means
    that we have found.
Seek not from them, those professing to be our confessors,
    but seek from ourselves
And will be found a day yet lived, a night yet come, to this
    our life can become.
Do not be confused, for seek and ye shall find.

Andrew Spencer

Grabbed

It's not surprising that people have thought
they could sail into paradise.
Distant islands rise misty and surreal;
the sun casts a silver road over the horizon.

After following this road through clear
blue waters and foaming sea swells
I found myself back on the shore
where I started.

The trees moved in the wind
and the seagulls soared over
the carved coastline.

While I want to believe
that love covers a multitude of sins,
I can't remember any of mine.

I still spend my time
staring into puddles trying
to catch a glimpse of the sky.

Driving across the Golden Gate Bridge
into the fog of nothingness,
an old zen master
grabbed me by the nose and said,
"what is this I have caught hold of?"

Caroline Misner

Mesa

The winds have sculpted these ancient stones
over a thousand years or more, the mountains
have burnished layers of crimson and ochre,
thrust from seas of dust, where Apache once
roamed these hallowed canyons.

The mesas rise like misshapen pillars
pushing against the dome of sky;
even at night they retain the sun, harboring
heat within their pulsing hearts, hot as a scorpion's
sting, in defiance of the dark.

My feet burn as I step upon its summit;
on the precipice of time, I stand poised
for flight. I call the sacred eagles to carry me
into the burgeoning sky, blue as the turquoise beads
the Hopi sell to tourists like me.

The wind is patient. It can wait another
thousand years to shape the stone and erode
these arid walls to sand, sand that spirals
and swirls like frenzied mists and covers
the calcified husks of the dead.

I step away from this craggy ledge and sacrifice
myself to the desert air. I needn't wings
or feathers to fly; I plunge and dissipate and become
a feast for lizards and rattlesnakes;
let them dwell within my shattered bones.

Rob Schultz

Perspective

Simple paradigm of perspective—
parallel lines that come together
in the distance, but never do
as train tracks receding from view.
Another trick played on the eye
that doesn't fool.
Lines of memory—history—
coterminous lives plotted on
parallel time lines—as we two—
may seem to come together too;
but it is only horizon or
last bend of a stream that runs
to the sea and infinity.
Even in this dim room a fire
flickers, center of all,
always, horizon and moon and sun
and stars here beside us.
To imagine peace and contentment
and absence of fear in the future
is to live it now,
is to live backward in time.

David Riddle

Returning

As if the plane had crashed
she walks across the tarmac,
jigsawed.

Leprous flesh trailing after her
the white satin train she had planned
now unplanned.

Uniform cleaned, pressed, hanging in the dark.
Showering day and night, bloody water swirling away
she drips friends and figures unknown

into the carpet, invisible stains. If she could cry
the desert wind would pull her tears across the salty ocean
falling on the cheeks of disembodied heads.

He stands with flowers and a ring.

She hugs coldly, embracing the rituals of returning
like holding an asp. Her blue lips kiss
chilling love, expectations, road maps to Texas.

New houses and white fences deep in ash
the snowfall of death. Pretending she is again flowing
along the river of life

she reads of new brides with a death row diligence.
She plays a game, spinning the cylinder
adding a new bullet after each click, stacking the odds.

He stands with flowers and a ring.

Mother, father look at pictures of a little girl
pink dress, Easter hat, Spring bright
stalked by sand covered trapdoors

opening onto a scene of Paradise Lost.
One piece preserved in a frame, others
scattered, lost, burning on the roadside.

Now less than the sum of the whole, bridesmaids
placed against the wall, soon slump to the ground
feeding the dust. She is as light as a word

floating around, driven by things she carves into stone
and hides under the bed that is cold on both sides.
Only a few broken pieces lie under the covers.

Glue, tape, words whispered on a couch, noted
on a pad, not enough is left to repair. Her once beautiful
body is a canvas with screaming bulls.

He stands with flowers and a ring.

No longer do memories of promises linger,
the future has been devoured by dust devils
hopping from dune to gun to soul. As she talks

sand falls from her words, drying what little
she can say to him. Truth needs water, stories
must eat of the sun; she breastfeeds

mouths that can no longer drink, eyes
rolled back looking inside, finding nothing.
Her soul is a shadow, black, and cringing

fearful to stand next to her; it wants to hide.
Embracing darkness, she hopes to keep
the light of the searching sun from revealing

what only she knows. Horror committed
sin enjoyed without shame; she is covered
with blood and sex, smelling of treachery

and slaughter. Singularity brings no solace
only less remembering. Memory is a gun
in an open mouth, a flower squeezing the trigger

a diamond bullet rushing down the barrel.

Amorak Huey

The Ethnomusicologist
& The Blackfoot Chief

The dark vowels of your eyes crave & curl
& say only nothing, only everything.
I catch myself expecting the sky

to walk in & spill your secrets. Perhaps
I never was supposed to fall in love
but your face is prairie upon which gold lingers

& the mood of this place is hopeful:
irresistible smell of hot ashes
& disappearing weather.

There is dirt on the hem of my sensible skirt.
To write, to celebrate, to predict.
To interpret means to condescend—

forgive me. All I ask
is the sharing: the wheatgrass, the forget-me-not.
From a certain angle, history

is mutable as wax cylinder,
miraculous as box camera—
this transcription of light & song.

Sophia Boettcher

The Toll of Unconscious Industrial Progression on the Environment: Examining Silicon's Growing Value and Our Continued Oil Dependency

I

Lo! I watched a chrome-hue smog
engulf the skies, burning as a torch;
the skies, which were His Pacific blue throne,
became as fire and hyacinth and brimstone.
Indeed, it seemed a new epoch
inherited the earth.

And as it were a wildfire kindled
by wind and thirsty trees—this new,
chrome-hue epoch blew
across all things, consuming the tender grass censer
arrayed with dew.

II

The watchful dreaded, No.
Nevermore.
Lightning among gloaming
cloudbursts and great hail
lit their eyes as candles,
whose flames were puffed in shadows.
Old oaks fell to shivers;
we took their flesh for doors.
When the lions ceased to roar
and the eagles did not soar,
the watchful uttered, Nevermore.

But, enraptured by the dusk
that overtook the air—
the intrepid carried forth
their plans,
holding firm for evermore.
They thrust in-
to the earth with blades,
whose hilts were girt with starry sparks.
The blades burnished rims of clouds
that looked like unto golden shrouds.

III
Sand leapt in a furnace
with burning coke and ashes,
all alight like magic.
They enkindled something new,
something tinged with blue
and full of crystalline faces—
twinkling and chrome-hue.

Oil came up thro' wells
on land and ocean floors,
dark as sack-cloth of goat hair.
We tore our robes in despair,
because the intrepid
could not hear
the screams of whales, cranes
or polar bears.
Woe! And Behemoth found no grass to eat;
rivers grew too shallow and unclean
for It to drink.

IV
Unrelenting, the intrepid raised their towers,
chanting, Hosanna, It is come.
It is coming.
Silicon had they for bricks
and oil—for mortar.

Behold! the dead animals
looked as if to say. Silicon and oil
have voices like unto trumpets
and teeth as fearsome teeth of Leviathan.
...hosanna, It is coming.

Peter Serchuk

The Ledge

Shall we be dazzled or afflicted?
she asked, the eye of the moon
half-shut, a new century of men
already defending their right to die.
She was twenty years younger
and I was out on the ledge where
the ground no longer seems visible
and men lose their fear of heights.
But I knew the ground, had walked
barefoot on its nails and prayed for
mercy to a God no longer visible.
The ground was no place to live
or love, and everything above
a dangerous illusion.
I had my own illusions, no need
of the ventriloquists insisting we
march the long road to paradise.
Dazzled or afflicted? The price
of failure clear enough. I kissed her
as if she were my only hope,
my only way of saying, *Both*.

Nickie Albert

Untitled

Nothing is off limits.
Nothing is too taboo, too mundane.
With a word done right, a preposition placed
for dramatic impact, an adroit adjective,
anything can be described.

The morning light on some verdant valley,
layers of hazy mist obscure the true view,
green and purple hills.

This coffee table with pock marks and cup rings
has a story of moving from place to place
and its origins, the ping of an old lover
in a sore heart.

A photograph of two fellows walking arm in arm
on a cobblestone street in the New York of our dreams.
A city where light was a commodity
and the object to dodge when traversing the streets
was horse shit.

A disquieting admission, muddy and hidden
inside the darkest heart, now come to the fore.
An orison of confession, an eloquent gush
of avowal and truth.

Any plant in full bloom, any rose
or tulip, that harbinger we confiscate with the lens,
the brush, the pen, opening the possibilities of scent
with the unsubtle hues of orange or yellow
or magenta.

Like the tulip, this poesy is a temporary performance,
a reel-to-reel of memoir and observation,
told with a flair that allows the ear to hear a note
different from any ever before.

Rachel Yu

This Gravity

A good way to fall in love is to drive
north on the old road, until the traffic

jams up, and the trucker in the soot-covered
18-wheeler taps his fingers restlessly

against the scratched dashboard. It's like
inside-out rain, and his truck is like the tractor

back between the bales on the farm, with the cow
that followed him everywhere, yes even when

it rained. Another good way to fall in love
is slowly. Suspended from the top of the London Eye,

the mischief-maker clambers to the edge
of the carriage and wonders why she never felt

this earth move before. And then the sky is dropping
slowly, and a flock of geese cackle across the Thames.

And then, a good way to fall in love is to fall
out of sync. The jet skiers know the salt

in the sea, and the dirt bikers know the rocks
better than the road. Between traffic lights, the trucker

smells hay in the golden farm and hears
the tinkering bells of the cow. This earth moves

a little, and the girl at the top of the world falls.

Joey Connelly

To a Lover Who Can't Sleep

No words, not now. Imagine instead
a meadow of lilacs: purple purring,
the sweet scent that calls the bees.

Just an image to appease:
a ride in a passenger seat. Calm can be
a compelling companion, but only at first,

like snow before bad roads turn the world
precarious. This skin around your ankle:
the thinnest, thinnest ice.

Or reflect Spring. Peer in your mirror
and see yellow sprouts. The delicate
spindle you have become. The tub your flowerpot:

sugar and cream and your cup
overflows: there's no practical purpose
for desire. Not here, not now.

Tongues of Pentecost inside you, lilacs:
beneath surfaces, you know what magpies know.

Close your filigree eyes: the darkness sharpens:
become your latest bruise.
Wake up purple.

Arfah Daud

While I Wait

Every afternoon, in the other room, my son
slowly and mournfully slices my heart
on the cello, stumbles on notes, stops, picks it up
again until it's time for us to meet the old
poets and writers we left on the shelves,
paper markers between the pages.

The books stand patient, waiting
for us to return to the story of Odysseus sailing
endlessly from Troy, delaying his journey home.

Every evening as we sit in the pale light
of the living room, I drown myself in Penelope's
sorrow as she weaves and unravels her web.
Impatiently I wait for my Odysseus
to come home from his journey across
several seas, the other side of the world.

Constantly on the move, he travels
back and forth every few months, delaying
his journey home for reasons unknown to me.
While I wait with growing impatience, upholding
sacred our union, my life hangs in limbo, eroding
with each passing day; the nights, lonelier.

It has taken him ten years to establish himself
in the business world, while I stumbled along
fitfully, picking up the pieces where we left off,
rolling and unrolling the yarn of our tapestry,
the bond we knitted years ago had loosened, threatens
to break from so much unraveling.

He's been home now, longer than usual.
Should he go or should he stay. I can't feel the
warmth of his body when his mind keeps wandering.
If it takes him another ten years to come,
will I wait?

Melissa Barrett

To a Sick Child

You may think it's all gone
unnoticed: your life
a voice, feeble

beneath a chorus, that no one
can hear you from under
the floorboards of disease.

You're here: saddled in a room
with walls so small and white
they fold down like little wings,

and the pleats of your little body
lay, soaking in the same
sun-starved clothes, hidden

between bedcovers. It's true
we don't know what you need.
We've forgotten

what childhood is. The sway
and candor of our moon, the great tilt
of the sky: completely feckless

for you, the one who grows
dizzy from staring.
But the pulse of the ocean

remains inside: teasing, lulling.
Close your eyes and read
the images there. These

are the true psalms, for in dreams
we unbolt the back door
and tiptoe out, to the far-off.

SPECIAL SECTION

Oklahoma American
Indian Authors

Contemporary American Indian Writers of Oklahoma: An Introduction to the Special Section of *New Plains Review*.

American Indian writers based in Indian Territory established an impressive body of literature more than a century ago. During the last forty years, their contemporary counterparts have expanded and have transformed the field of American Indian literature.

As a way of acknowledging the efforts of contemporary American Indian writers from Oklahoma, University of Central Oklahoma students researched and developed twenty-five profiles.

An assortment of iconic, established, and emerging voices, the individuals profiled in this issue include artists, dramatists, educators, essayists, fictionists, filmmakers, illustrators, novelists, poets, and storytellers.

In each instance, their realities, contributions, and accomplishments enhance our understanding of American Indian literature. Mvto.

Timothy Petete

Jim Barnes
(b. 1933)

Jim Barnes (Choctaw/Welsh) was raised in Summerfield, Oklahoma on the eastern edge of the Choctaw Nation that borders Arkansas. He taught Comparative Literature at Truman State University, and English at Brigham Young University. Barnes lives with his wife Cora, an accomplished artist and designer. Both call Santa Fe, New Mexico, and Atoka, Oklahoma, home.

Barnes founded the *Chariton Review* and was editor from 1975 to 2010. He is a contributing editor for the coveted *Pushcart Prize* and has been published in numerous journals that include *The Nation, Sewanee Review, The Chicago Review, Kenyon Review, The American Scholar, Georgia Review,* and the *Prairie Schooner.* Before his prestigious career as a poet and professor, Barnes attended Southeastern College in Durant, Oklahoma, where he received a Bachelor of Arts. He then went on to graduate with a Masters in 1965, as well as Ph.D. in 1972 from the University of Arkansas.

Barnes's contribution to the art of poetry includes *Visiting Picasso* (2008), *On a Wing of the Sun: Three Volumes of Poetry* (2002), *Paris: Poems* (1998), *The Sawdust War: Poems* (1993), *The La Plata Cantata: Poems* (1989), *A Season of Loss* (1985), *American Book of the Dead* (1982), *The Fish on Poteau Mountain* (1980), *This Crazy Land* (1980), and *Five Missouri Poets* (1979). His prose *On Native Ground: Memoirs and Impressions* (1997) gives readers vivid details and images of Oklahoma, as well as various places he has traveled.

Translated poetry won him the prominent Translation Prize in 1980 for his work *Summons and Signs: Poems* (1980) that reintroduced the poetry of German poet Dagmar Nick to the world. Barnes is also noted for being published in textbooks such as *250 Poems: A Portable Anthology* (2008), *Literature: A Portable Anthology* (2008), *The Mind's Eye: A Guide to Writing Poetry* (2007), *Approaching Poetry in the 21st Century* (2004), *Approaching Poetry: Perspectives and Responses* (1996), *Question and Form in Literature* (1982), and *Focus on Literature: Forms* (1978). Copious short stories and poems of his have been published in over 40 anthologies throughout his career.

Barnes enjoys travel, and during a recent interview mentioned fond memories of France and the Czech Republic. He said he was in Paris to "Stock up the image bank." Like a sponge he absorbed the great city. Quintessential imagery of Paris can be smelled, heard, and practically touched while reading his collection *Paris: Poems* (1998). Barnes was asked "What sort of advice do you give aspiring writers and students?" to which he genuinely replied "You are not the only one out there who thinks he has something to say. Be a reader. If you don't read you won't be a writer—only a scribbler."

Eddie Chuculate
(b. 1972)

Eddie Chuculate (Creek-Cherokee), was born in Claremore and raised in Muskogee. He has worked as a sports writer, copy editor, and columnist for almost two decades. He has also worked at several publications, including *The Tulsa World, The Denver Post,* and *The Albuquerque Tribune.*

Chuculate received a degree in creative writing at the Institute of American Indian Arts and held a Wallace Stegner creative writing fellowship at Stanford University. Currently, he is an MFA student at the Iowa Writers Workshop, a graduate-level creative writing program at the University of Iowa.

Chuculate's work is heavily influenced by personal experience and thus has a very poignant feel. His background as a Native American adds a unique feel to his work because of the different perspective that this influence brings to the table. This coupled with a one of a kind wry humor and commitment to not shying away from showing true human weakness in his characters makes Chuculate an author to be reckoned with.

His first book-length publication is *Cheyenne Madonna* (2010), a collection of short stories. His stories have also appeared in *New Plains Review, Blue Mesa Review, The Iowa Review, Manoa, The Kenyon Review, Many Mountains Moving, Ploughshares* and *Weber Studies.* Furthermore, he received the PEN/O. Henry Award in 2007 for his story 'Galveston Bay, 1826.'

Proof of his talents can be found in the 2010 July/August edition of *World Literature Today* where he was featured as their "Emerging Author." This shows his potential as an author and also that fact that perhaps his best work is still to come.

In a recent interview we learned that Chuculate took fifteen years to write *Cheyenne Madonna,* showing dedication and commitment. His most important and time consuming work is constructed of seven connected stories that follow a half-Cherokee adolescent who has to deal with a dysfunctional family and his desire to become an artist. This has a deep resonance with his personal life, which is partly why these stories are so powerful.

Amanda Cobb-Greetham

Amanda Cobb-Greetham is a writer, professor, and active member of the Chickasaw Nation of Oklahoma. Originally from Ardmore, Oklahoma, Dr. Cobb-Greetham comes from a long line of successful scholars.

Dr. Cobb-Greetham earned degrees at Southeastern Oklahoma State University (B.A., 1992), the University of North Texas (M.A., 1993), and the University of Oklahoma (Ph.D., 1997). She served as a professor at New Mexico State University and the University of New Mexico. While at the University of New Mexico, Dr. Cobb-Greetham also founded and served as the first director of the Institute for American Indian Research. She is a tenured associate professor at Oklahoma State University, specializing in Native American Studies. Dr. Cobb-Greetham is also the managing editor of *American Indian Quarterly*.

Currently, she is the director of the Chickasaw Division of History and Culture. She oversees the Chickasaw Nation's libraries, archives, language programs, the *Chickasaw Press*, and she recently oversaw the construction of the Chickasaw Cultural Center Complex completed in 2010 in Sulpher, Oklahoma.

Dr. Cobb-Greetham's work is concerned with preserving the rich heritage of the Chickasaw people. Her publications include *Listening to Our Grandmothers' Stories: The Bloomfield Academy for Chickasaw Females, 1852-1949* (2000), *Chickasaw: Unconquered and Unconquerable* (2006) with Jeannie Barbour and Linda Hogan, and *The National Museum of the American Indian: Critical Conversations* (2008) co-edited with Amy Lonetree.

Listening to Our Grandmothers' Stories won both the American Book Award and the North American Indian Prose Award, whereas *Chickasaw: Unconquered and Unconquerable* won two medals from the Independent Publishers Association.

Robert J. Conley
(b. 1940)

Robert J. Conley, who is of Cherokee descent, was born in Cushing, Oklahoma, in the land where the wild still ran free... where Western films were popular and almost everyone played "Cowboys and Indians... when a young Robert dreamed of becoming a cowboy movie star." This dream would eventually lead him to write about the Wild West and its many colorful characters.

He earned his bachelor's degree in Drama at Midwestern University in 1966 and his master's degree in English in 1968. Upon graduation, he became the Director of Indian Studies at Morningside College in Sioux City, Eastern Montana College, and Bacone College, Associate Professor in the English department at Morningside College, and Instructor of English at Northern Illinois University and Missouri State University. Since July 2008, he has been employed as a professor at Western Carolina University in Cherokee Studies. Conley writes both short stories and poems with his poems being published in not only English, but also in German, Cherokee, Macedonian, and French.

His first poem "Some Lines in commemoration of this site: Little Maquoketa River Mounds," was published in 1981 and began his literary career. When he moved out of state and began to reflect on Oklahoma, it's history, and it's infamous people, he began to write about his home state. He believed the accounts of Ned Christie were incorrect and desired to find research which could correct those mistakes. This research inspired him to write his first novel, *Back to Malachi*, which was published in 1986. The *Real People Series* is based on well-known Native Americans and includes the books *The Way of the Priests* (1992), *War Woman* (1997), *The Peace Chief (1998), The Dark Island* (2000), and *Cherokee Dragon* (2000). His novel, *Cherokee Thoughts: Honest and Uncensored* (2008) is a candid look at what it means to be Cherokee. His favorite short story is "Plastic Indian," in which a group of Cherokee men desire to eliminate the presence of a large plastic Indian in front of a store. This is an often seen sight at Indian Trading Posts in the 1960s and 1970s. His favorite author is Max Evans, a popular author of Western literature, of whom he reads regularly. His down to earth attitude is most reflected by his recollection of his most cherished memory—the day when his wife Evelyn said "yes."

Conley's prestigious honors have been abundant. He was inducted into the Oklahoma Professional Writers Hall of Fame in 1996 and was the Oklahoma Writer of the Year in 1999. His work, *Cherokee Medicine Man*, was nominated for the Oklahoma Reads Program in 2007, and *The Cherokee Nation: A History* was selected as one of the Outstanding Academic Titles of the Year in 2000. Mr. Conley is a talented man whose written words will intrigue all who have the privilege of reading him... both present and future generations.

Santee Frazier
(b. 1978)

Santee Frazier is an Oklahoma Cherokee Nation citizen. In Santa Fe, NM, at the Institute of American Indian Arts, he earned a Bachelor of Fine Arts degree. He then furthered his education at Syracuse University, where he received a Master of Fine Arts degree in Creative Writing. While earning his BFA degree, he studied under the poets Arthur Sze and Jon Davis. When he was at Syracuse University he developed his thesis, which was *Dark Thirty*.

Dark Thirty was Santee Frazier's first collection of poems. In 2009, The University of Arizona Press released them. *Dark Thirty* is not the typical poetic writings most people think of when they read poetry. They come from a darker place of mixed emotions and real-life situations. The poems' tough and uncanny subject matter is portrayed elegantly through the use of Frazier's original style. With his marvelous use of description and imagery, it seems as if the settings described in his poems are places we have actually visited before.

As a cultured, talented, and educated man from the Cherokee Nation, Santee packs his poems with a lot of emotion and memories from the past. The way he uses such vivid descriptions and mind-blowing details are what keeps his readers on the edge of their seats; it leaves them wanting to come back for more.

He has been a visiting poet at Santa Fe Indian School, White Horse High School, and Dine College. He was a teaching assistant at Syracuse University during the 2007-2008 school year. While at Syracuse University, he taught Academic Writing to freshman- and sophomore-level students. He was also a Visiting Poetry Instructor at the Downtown Writers Center in both the Spring 2010 and Fall 2010 semesters.

His poetry is published in several journals, including *The Ontario Review, American Poet, Oregon Literary Review, Many Mountains Moving, To Topos, Narrative Magazine,* and *Third Coast.*

He has received many awards for his works. Back in 2001, he received a full scholarship from the Naropa Summer Writing Undergraduate Scholarship and the full Truman Capote Scholarship from the Institute of American Indian Arts in the Creative Writing Program.

In 2005, he earned a full scholarship from Idyllwild Summer Poetry and in 2006, a full scholarship from Napa Valley Writers' Workshop. He also earned a full scholarship in the summer program from The Fine Arts Work Center's Archie D. and the Bertha H. Walker Scholarship in 2007. From 2006-2009, he earned full fellowship in a Creative Writing program from Syracuse University.

In 2009, he earned the Lannan Foundation Residency Fellowship. His most recent award includes The School for Advanced Research Indigenous Writer-in-Residence Fellowship in 2011.

Diane Glancy

(b. 1941)

Diane Glancy, an author of both German and Cherokee heritage, was born in Kansas City, Missouri in 1941. "Knowing the need to develop thoughts and ideas through education," she earned a Bachelor of Arts degree in English Literature from the University of Missouri in 1964. She later continued her education at the University of Central Oklahoma earning her Masters of the Arts degree in 1983. She received a Master of Fine Arts degree from the University of Iowa Writer's Workshop in 1988.

A professor of English, she taught Native American Literature and Creative Writing for nearly two decades at Macalester College in St. Paul, Minnesota. Likewise, she taught in the Bread Loaf School of English Master of Art program at the Native American Preparatory School in Rowe, New Mexico. In the years 2008 through 2009, she held the prestigious Visiting Richard Thomas Chair at Kenyon College, as well as the "Title of Artist in Residence" for the States Arts Council of Oklahoma for almost ten years.

The recipient of countless awards and nominations, she received the 1984 Pegasus Award from the Oklahoma Federation of Writers for her collection, *Brown Wolf Leaves the Res and Other Poems*. Shortly after, Glancy was named laureate for the Five Civilized Tribes from the year 1984 to 1986. She received the 1987 Five Civilized Tribes Playwriting Prize for her play *Weebjob*. In 1993, she received the Emily Dickinson Poetry Prize from the Poetry Society of America, and her piece *Iron Woman* captured the Capricorn prize, given by The Writers Voice of New York. Glancy was awarded Writer of the Year for Screenplays through the years 2003-2004 by the Wordcraft Circle of Native Writers and Storytellers. In 2003, she received a grant from National Endowment for the Arts, the Oklahoma Book Award for fiction for her piece, *The Mask Maker*. Her collection, *Primer of the Obsolete*, earned the 2003 Juniper Prize for Poetry; she also received the Cherokee Medal of Honor and Cherokee Honor Society for her countless accomplishments. In 2006, she received the Distinguished Alumni Award from the University of Central Oklahoma. A year later, Glancy received the Multi-Arts Production grant by the Creative Capital Foundation and Rockefeller Foundation. She recently received the Expressive Arts grant from the National Museum of the American Indian in 2009.

An award winning poet, play write, essayist, short story writer, novelist, and author of more than thirty books, Glancy has captured the heart of America with her ability to combine oral tradition with sacred meaning. Her most recent writing, *In-between Places*, is a collection of eleven essays exploring the middle region of concern of cross-cultural issues of language and their relation to both landscape and spiritual life (2004). Her recent short story collection, *The Dance Partner: Stories of the Ghost Dance*, takes you back through a historical perspective of the Ghost Dance and its symbolization to the Native American people (2005). *The Reason for Crows: A Story of Kateri Tekakwitha* (2009), is Glancy's third novel of a series following *Pushing Bear: A Novel of the Trail of Tears* (1996) and *Stone Heart: A Novel of Sacajawea* (2003), each centered on woman by the name of Kateri Tekakwitha. Glancy captures the inner identity of this woman struggling with momentous change and pushing herself to overcome obstacles of an ever-changing life. In her recent poetry collection, *Asylum in the Grassland*, she searches the hearts of the Cherokee people and explores the losses of a world past as a new world approaches (2006). Glancy has left her thumbprint in life by "Giving voice to historical characters that did not have their chance to speak." Her words have been an inspiration to many, and her work will continue to encourage for years to come.

Leslie D. Hannah
(b. 1961)

Dr. Leslie D. Hannah is a Wolf Clan Cherokee from Stillwell, Oklahoma. He acquired a Bachelor of Arts degree and a Master of Science degree from Northeastern State University. He received a doctorate in English at the University of Oklahoma.

Hannah frequently lectures and performs at storytelling conferences, symposiums, academic conferences, and academic institutions.

His academic publications include "Kill the Indian—Save the Man?" (1998), *Discovering Your Vision and Voice* (2011), and *Engage* (2011). His creative publications include *In the Spirit of Tahlequah: Ghost Stories from the Cherokee Nation* (1996), "The Trees" (1997), "The Maples and the Oaks" (2001), *Seven and Seven* (2004), and "The Day the Little Deer Said Thank You" (2008). His poems include "Deep in the Forest" (1994), "Spirit of a Warrior" (1998), and "With a Drink and a Friend".

He completed a residency at Oxford University in 2007. During this time, he also addressed the World Universities Forum in Davos, Switzerland. In 2010, Hannah served as a Fulbright scholar. He taught Native American Studies at Esbjerg Handleskole.

Hannah has taught English, Native American Literature, and American Literature courses at many institutions: the University of Oklahoma, Kansas State University, Louisiana State University, and Loyola Marymount University.

He is an active member of the Wordcraft Circle of Native American Writers and Storytellers, the American Association of University Professors, the National Council of Teachers of English, the Modern Language Association, and Sigma Tau Delta.

Currently, Hannah serves as Chair of the Languages and Literature Department and Director of the Language and Studies Program at Northeastern State University.

Joy Harjo
(b. 1951)

Born in Tulsa, Joy Harjo attended boarding school in Santa Fe, where her love and talent for writing was first recognized. In later life, Harjo completed her degree at the University of New Mexico in 1976 and continued her education by achieving her Master of Fine Arts at the University of Iowa. She has taught at the University of Colorado, the University of Arizona, and the University of California, Los Angeles. In addition, she has taken part in a Filmmaking Program at the Anthropology Film Center.

Harjo's work is popular around the world and is used in literature courses and published in anthologies, but she claims that her main audience is the people within her "tribal nation." Leslie Ullman claims that Harjo's work "restores vitality to culture at large" and Harjo believes that writing helps her to share stories and the lessons she has learned throughout her life, a tradition which is important to her tribe.

Her collections of poetry are *The Last Song* (1975), *What Moon Drove Me to This?* (1979), *Secrets From the Center of the World* (1989), *In Mad Love and War* (1990), *Fishing* (1991), *The Woman Who Fell From the Sky* (1994) and *The Spiral of Memory* (1996). More recent additions are *Reinventing the Enemy's Language* (1997), *The Good Luck Cat* (2000), *A Map Next to the World* (2000), *How We Became Human* (2003), *She Had Some Horses* (2008) and *For A Girl Becoming* (2009).

Harjo's other work include music, and her CDs include *Red Dreams: A Trail Beyond Tears, Winding Through the Milky Way, She Had Some Horses, Native Joy For Real* and *Letters from the End of the 20th Century*. Harjo plays the saxophone and has co-produced some plays, such as *I Think I Love You: An All Night Round Dance* and *Wings of Night Sky, Wings of Morning Light*. She has created a video diary and narrated *Games of the North: Playing for Survival*. Harjo co-directed and co-produced *Eagle Song*, her first music video, which was nominated for an award at the 2002 Native American Indian Film and Video Festival. She also co-wrote and co-produced *A Thousand Roads* (2005).

Harjo has earned a variety of awards for her works, including Best Live Short, American Indian Film Festival, Award of Excellence for Best Feature Film, Indian Summer Image Awards, Best Dramatic Film, Native Voice Festival and Best Short Drama, Winnipeg Aboriginal Film and Video Festival. In 2011, she received the Mvskoke Women's Leadership Award (Artist of the Year).

Stuart "Sy" Hoahwah
(b. 1973)

Stuart "Sy" Hoahwah was born in Little Rock, Arkansas. His family descends from Yapaituka/Penatuka Comanche and Bad Faces band of Southern Arapaho. Hoahwah was raised in Arkansas and southwestern Oklahoma. He is a direct descendent of Comanche principal chief Ten Bears as well as Arapaho leader, Little Raven.

Hoahwah received his Bachelors degree from the University of Arkansas at Little Rock, attended Oklahoma State University, and earned a Master of Fine Arts from the University of Arkansas. A multitalented writer and painter, Hoahwah's career first began as a virtual artist, where he discovered his talent and began working with acrylic paint. It was not until 1994, after his mother's death, that a turning point in expression and purpose occurred. He began seriously writing and found that his strongest gift was poetry.

He is considered to be both a Native American and Southern poet, due to his works being heavily influenced by his heritage. His works carry a powerful sense of Comanche culture, with an overlying theme of his Southern heritage. Hoahwah's work *Black Knife* was discussed and used as a course book for an American Literature course at the University of Albuquerque. His use of oral traditions, realities, culture, imagery, and his goal to dispose traditions of American Indian subjects such as reservations, victimizations, and removal illustrates why he is considered one of the well-known authors of the contemporary American Indian culture.

In 2001, through the University of Louisiana, a collection of Hoahwah's poetry was published in a chapbook titled *Split*. Four years later, in 2005, the University of Arkansas at Little Rock published a second poetry chapbook *Black Knife*. His latest work *Velroy and the Madischie Mafia* that was published in 2009, took over 10 years before it was completed. His poems are fiction based with underlying truth to the Comanche tribe. They are complex imagistic, gang subculture, witchcraft, and ghost tradition fused in narratives, reconstructing Comanche mythology with contemporary shape of cultural evolution. Kimberly Blaeser, a Chippewa Native American writer, said "In a remarkable poetic gesture, Hoahwah's book echoes our own 'hunger to answer' old languages heard in the dark."

Hoahwah received the Certificate of Appreciation from the Office of Indian Education Program (1996). He also received The Alma K. Dougherty Award (1996). He has been an active member of Academy of American Poets since 1998. He currently resides near St. Louis, Missouri, with his wife and five children.

Linda Hogan

(b. 1947)

Linda Hogan (Chickasaw) was born in Denver, Colorado. As a child, Hogan was raised in a military family and moved around quite often. She taught at the University of Colorado in the English Department in Boulder; she received her M.A. there in 1978.

Hogan did not always want to become a writer. It was not until her late twenties that she realized she could write. Along with writing, Hogan is passionate about the environment. Her love of the environment is also incorporated in her writing and greatly influences it.

Hogan is a novelist, poet, essayist and playwright. There have also been many anthologies containing her work. She also wrote the geography books *Sightings, The Mysterious Journey of the Gray Whale* along with Brenda Peterson.

Her novels include *Mean Spirit* (1990), *Solar Storms* (1995), *Dwellings, A Spiritual History of the Land* (1995), *Power* (1998), *The Women Who Watches Over the World: A Native Memoir* (2001), *People of the Whale* (2008) and *Rounding the Human Corners* (2008).

Her poetry collections include *Calling Myself Home* (1978), *Daughters, I Love You* (1981), *Eclipse* (1983), *Seeing Through the Sun* (1985), *Savings* (1988), *Red Clay* (1991), and *The Book of Medicines* (1993). She also published a collection of essays, *The Inner Journey: Native Traditions*, and a collection of plays, *Everything Has a Script, A Piece of Moon* (1981).

When Hogan isn't writing she likes to spend time with animals. She takes care of eagles, hawks, owls, and mustangs. She also likes to sing to the animals in her native language when working with them. She has also been involved with the Native Science Dialogues, the new Native American Academy and the SEED Graduate Institute in Albuquerque for many years.

She has received many awards for her works. She garnered an Oklahoma Book Award for fiction and The Mountains and Plains Book Award for fiction (for *Mean Spirit*). She received two Colorado Book awards (for *The Book of Medicines and for Solar Storms*). She earned a Five Civilized Tribes Playwriting Award (for *A Piece of the Moon*) and an American Book Award (for *Seeing Through the Sun*).

Hogan also received a Lifetime Achievement Award from the Native Writers' Circle of the Americas and from The Mountains and Plains Booksellers Association. In 2007, she was inducted into the Chickasaw Nation Hall of Fame.

Hogan is currently the Writer-in-Residence for The Chickasaw Nation Division of Arts and Humanities.

Sara Sue Hoklotubbe

Sara Sue Hoklotubbe was born in Oklahoma and raised near Lake Eucha located in the northeast part of the state. Hoklotubbe, a member of the Cherokee Nation tribe, bases her work around her heritage. She graduated from Oklahoma University, but found her calling while enrolled in a six-week writing class at a local community college.

Hoklotubbe's family has influenced her greatly in her journey of writing. Her story telling skills were inherited. Her father "could tell the greatest fish story in Delaware County" as quoted from her personal website. Hoklotubbe's grandmother also inspired her, spurring on her passion for the Cherokee people and culture.

Her mystery-fiction series is created around the lifestyle Hoklotubbe loves. The setting for the books is located in the place she called home. Ideally, she wishes to reach her readers with an exciting and entertaining story while sharing the Cherokee culture with them as well.

Hoklotubbe's novel *Deception on All Accounts* (2003) features her character Sadie Walela, who is half Cherokee, facing a mystery on her hands as well as trying to discover herself. Hoklotubbe's most recent novel *The American Café* (2011) is the sequel in the Sadie Walela series.

Hoklotubbe was named Writer of the Year by Wordcraft Circle of Native Writers for her first novel, *Deception*. She is a member of many writing groups which include Oklahoma Writers' Federation, Inc., Mystery Writers of America, Tulsa Night Writers, and Sisters in Crime.

Judith Houston Emerson

Former high school English teacher, Judith Houston Emerson is an enrolled member of the Cherokee Nation of Oklahoma. Not only is Emerson the creative mind behind her novel *Myth Makers* (2010), she is also an extraordinary visual artist with experience in sculpture, painting, and drawing.

Education has been of predominate importance to Emerson. Apart from her career as an English teacher, she has designed and taught a seminar at the University of Central Oklahoma on Indian Art History. In addition, Emerson has judged a range of art competitions, taught drawing classes, and held her own Open Studio drawing groups in Oklahoma City.

Emerson spent four years studying sculpture, drawing, and art history in Florence, Italy. Following her studies in Florence, Emerson was awarded a scholarship in drawing at the Art Students League in New York where she studied sculpture, painting, and drawing. She also attended the Academy of Realist Art in Santa Fe, New Mexico, and more recently she studied painting in La Coste, France.

In 1997, Emerson was employed by the Smithsonian National Museum of the American Indian. After which, she returned to her home state of Oklahoma to work as a consultant for Philbrook Museum and the Cherokee Museum.

Currently, Emerson is active in the National Audabon Society, the Tulsa Nitewriters, the Oklahoma Jazz Society, the Native American Alumni Society of Northeastern State University, and the Art Students League of New York.

More recently Emerson has completed The Chisholm Trail Book Festival in Duncan, Oklahoma (2011) and she is currently gathering local Native American actors to shoot a scene from her novel. Future plans consist of finishing *The Teller and the Told* (the sequel to *Myth Makers*), illustrating a children's book, and writing a memoir.

LeAnne Howe
(b. 1951)

LeAnne Howe, American Indian author and scholar, was born in Edmond, Oklahoma. She grew up in Oklahoma City and is a member of the Choctaw Nation of Oklahoma. She currently teaches at the University of Illinois in both the American Indian Studies and Creative Writing programs. As an author and scholar she has travelled the world lecturing and reading selections of her own work.

Howe's career started as a mix of writing and business. From the late 1970s through 1989 Howe worked as a newspaper journalist for the Dallas Morning News, simultaneously selling bonds on Wall Street throughout the mid 1980s. As time progressed she began to lean toward academics and started teaching, even creating Native American Studies courses at Carleton College in Minnesota and the University of Iowa.

Howe has quite an impressive collection of work including novels, short fiction, essays, and anthologies; she has also been involved in five theater productions and a radio production that she wrote and directed called "Indian Radio Days." Her works include the novels *Coyote Stories* (1984), *A Stand Up Reader* (1987), *Shell Shaker* (2001), and *Miko Kings: An Indian Baseball Story* (2007), as well as the short fiction pieces "An American in New York" (1989), "Evidence of Red" (1994), and "Indians Never Say Good-Bye" (1997) just to name a few. Howe also co-produced "Playing Pastime" with Jim Fortier which is a 30 minute documentary on American Indian baseball leagues in Oklahoma.

Howe is no stranger to recognition and achievement. She was the recipient of an American Book Award for her novel *Shell Shaker*. In 2006 *Evidence of Red* received The Oklahoma Book Award for poetry. In 2003 Howe was selected as the Louis D. Roubins Jr. Writer-in-Residence at Hollins University in Virginia, and in 2006 she was selected as the John and Renee Grisham Writer-in-Residence at the University of Mississippi. Most recently, Howe was awarded the Tulsa Winning Library Trust's American Indian Words Award and she was a 2010-2011 Fulbright Scholar.

Navarre Scott Momaday
(b. 1934)

Navarre Scott Momaday was born at the Kiowa Indian hospital in Lawton, Oklahoma. Momaday's father was a Kiowa artist and painter whose mother was part Cherokee, working as an educator for the Bureau of Indian Affairs. When Navarre was barely a year old, the couple moved to New Mexico and later Arizona, where they taught for reservation schools.

When describing his childhood, Momaday, one of the Nation's most prolific writers, scholars, and educators, recalls how he straddled two worlds growing up. Momaday was not only exposed to the Kiowa traditions of his father's family, but also to the traditions of the Navajo, Apache, and Pueblo tribes he was immersed in growing up on reservations in the Southwest, and the adjacent cultures of White and Hispanic settlers. Momaday's diverse upbringing helped shape his strong impression of pan-indianism, a movement within his writing that embraced the unity among different Native American groups regardless of their tribal affiliation. Momaday's diverse upbringing also contributed considerably to his love for American literature.

He received his B.A. at the University of New Mexico and his M.A. and Ph.D. at Stanford University. Throughout his academic career, Momaday was considered a reputed scholar for his research and coursework on Emily Dickinson and Frederick Goddard Tuckerman, as well as his studies in Indian oral traditions.

Momaday's writing emphasizes the importance of the Kiowa landscape and traditions, drawing upon stories and myths he heard as a child for the poignant subject matter of his novels and poetry— primarily pulling from the memories and stories of his mother and father. Momaday's writing emphasizes the healing power of Native American traditions, reconnecting Native American characters back to their tribal heritages as a means to mediate the internal conflicts caused by assimilation and marginalization. His writing also celebrates the multiethnic and multicultural experience of the Native American experience.

Scott Momaday's most notable works of prose include *House*

Made of Dawn (1968), *The Way to Rainy Mountain* (1969), *The Names: A Memoir* (1976), and *The Ancient Child* (1989). Momaday's collections of poetry include *Angle Geese and Other Poems* (1974), *The Gourd Dancer* (1976), *In the Presence of the Sun* (1992), and *In the Bear's House* (1999).

Momaday has received many commendations throughout his prolific career and is regarded as one of the Nation's most prominent writers. His honors include: a Fellowship to Stanford University, the Pulitzer Prize for Fiction (for *House Made of Dawn*), the Golden Plate Award from the American Academy of Achievement, honors from the National Institute of Arts and Letters, an Academy of American Poets Prize; the National Medal of Arts, and the Premio Letterario Internationale "Mondello," the highest literary award of Italy.

In addition, Momaday holds honorary degrees at over 12 universities, is the poet laureate of Oklahoma Centennial, and sits as a chair on the Board of First Nations Development Institute and Research.

Carter Revard
(b. 1931)

Carter Revard was born in the Indian Agency town of Pawhuska, Oklahoma. His father is of Osage descent, while his mother is of Scottish and Irish heritage. In 1952 he received his Osage name, Nompehwahteh, which means "fear-inspiring," from his grandmother, Mrs. Josephine Jump.

He was raised on the Osage Reservation and attended Buck Creek School—a one-room schoolhouse with eight different grades of students. Revard, along with having a twin sister, grew up with four other brothers and trained dogs and worked on a farm.

Revard received his high school diploma from Bartlesville College High and went on to win a scholarship from a radio quiz to the University of Tulsa. He received his B.A. from the University of Tulsa in 1952 while also receiving a Rhodes Scholarship which he used to earn his second B.A. at Oxford University. Following Oxford University, he attended Yale University where he received his PhD. His concentrations of study were in Linguistics, Medieval English Literature, and American Indian Literature. Revard has taught at both Amherst College in Amherst, Massachusetts, and Washington University in St. Louis, Missouri, the latter of which he retired from teaching in 1997.

He has published two anthologies: his *Ponca War Dancers* (1980) and *Cowboys and Indians Christmas Shopping* (1992). Some of his other publications include *An Eagle Nation* (1997), *Family Matters* (1999), *Winning the Dust Bowl* (2001), and *How the Songs Come Down* (2005). Revard is the editor of *Native Heritage: American Indian Literature* (1993). His work is also published in seventeen anthologies.

Revard has received several awards for his poetry and prose. In 1994, he won the Oklahoma Book Award for *An Eagle Nation*. Revard was also a two-time finalist for the Oklahoma Book Award for *Winning the Dust Bowl and Family Matters, Tribal Affairs*. He received the Writer of the Year award in 2000 from the Wordcraft Circle of Native Writers. He received the organization's Lifetime Achievement Award in 2005.

He is a member of the Modern Language Association, the River Styx Literary Organization, the Association for Studies in American Indian Literature, the University of Tulsa Board of Visitors, the Association of American Rhodes Scholars, Phi Beta Kappa and the St. Louis Gourd Dancers.

Revard continues to write, give poetry readings, and do scholarly work in Middle English Literature, Manuscript Studies, and American Indian Literature. In June 2011, he had a writing residency at the Chateau de Lavigny in Switzerland where he worked on his new collection of poems entitled *From the Extinct Volcano, A Bird of Paradise*. He and his wife, Stella, a Milton scholar, have been currently doing scholarly work at the British Library in London, England. There, he worked on an essay called "Milton as a Muse for Keats, Shelley, and Robert Frost." Two of his poems, "Deer Mice Singing Up the Parnassus" and "Æsculapius Unbound" are set to be published in an anthology from the University of Arizona Press called *SING: Poetry from the Indigenous Americas*. He also has an essay from a conference held at the University of East Anglia in July 2009 set to be published by SUNY Press next year entitled, "Tumblebuggery, Creation Stories, The Birth of a Nation, and Globalistics."

Kimberly Roppolo

Kimberly Roppolo was born in Baytown, Texas. She is of mixed heritage, including Cherokee, Choctaw and Creek ancestry. She has three children: Cody, 26, Rachel, 22, and Marley, 13. Her middle child is autistic, which has added another dimension to her family's lives.

Roppolo is an Assistant Professor of English and a faculty member affiliated with the Native American Studies department at the University of Oklahoma. She was also an Assistant Professor of Native Studies at the University of Lethbridge in Lethbridge, Alberta, Canada for four years. She earned her B.A., M.A., and Ph.D. at Baylor University in Waco, Texas. Roppolo is the former National Director and current Vice President of the Wordcraft Circle of Native Writers and Storytellers. She is also the co-author of the University of Oklahoma Press book, *Reasoning Together: The Native Critics Collective* (2008).

Roppolo has written and published poems, articles, book reviews, and reference entries for anthologies and publications. These anthologies and publications include *Studies in American Indian Literatures*, *American Indian Quarterly*, *News from Indian Country* and *Talking Stick Arts Newsletter*. Roppolo's areas of interest are contemporary Native Literatures, Native Critical Theories, Women's Literature, Native Rhetoric, and Native Creative Writing.

Roppolo's awards include the Christine Fall Teaching Award from the Baylor University Department of English, Wordcraft Circle Academic Research Paper of the Year, Wordcrafter of the Year, Native Writers Circle of the Americas (for *Back to the Blanket: Reading, Writing, and Resistance for American Indian Literary Critics*) and Wordcraft Circle Storyteller Award for Performance of the Year (for *The Fall*).

William "Sundown" Sanders
(b. 1942)

Williams Sanders is a retired Cherokee writer who lives in Tahlequah, Oklahoma. He is best known for his speculative fiction but has also written mysteries, thrillers and even histories. *Journey to Fusang* (1988) and *The Wild Blue and the Gray* (1991) are two of his popular alternative history novels. His speculative fiction/adventure novels include *Pockets of Resistance* (1990), *The Hellbound Train* (1990), *Steel Wings* (1991), *Hardball* (1992), *Aryan Legion* (1992), *Skorpion* (1992) and *J.* (2001). His mystery novels include *The Next Victim* (1993), *A Death on 66* (1994), *Smoke* (1994) and *Blood Autumn* (1995). He has also written the thriller novels *The Ballad of Billy Badass and The Rose of Turkestan* (1999) and *The Bernadette Operation* (2001).

Sanders initially enjoyed his retirement by reading and traveling. After a while he returned to the world of speculative fiction, starting the magazine *Helix* alongside friends and colleagues. He has received several honors and awards for his writing, including being a finalist for the John W. Campbell Award in 1988 and Oklahoma Book Award in 1993 and 1994. He won the Sidewise Award for Alternative History in 1998 and 2003.

Michael Sheyashe
(b.1975)

Michael Sheyahshe (Caddo) graduated *cum laude* from The University of Oklahoma in 2003. He received a BA in Native American Studies and a BA in Film and Video Studies. In 2011, Sheyahshe received his MFA in 3d Modeling from the Academy of Art Institute.

In 1998, as a freshman at OU, Sheyahshe was selected as an intern at the National Museum of American History in Washington, DC. He also received the Smithsonian Institution Native American Award.

Some if his interests include 3D Modeling, 3D Animation, video games, comic books, simulation, and representing Native Americans. As a result, he now owns and operates alterNative Media. In addition to running alterNative Media, Sheyahshe is a former Tax Commissioner for the Caddo Nation and has been previously appointed a seat on the Board of Trustees for the Caddo Heritage Museum.

In 2008, Sheyahshe's first book *Native American's in Comic Books* was published by McFarland Publications. He has been published in many magazines including *Illusions, Trauma Magazine, Native People Magazine*, and *Games for Windows*. Putting his artistic talent to use, he has achieved many awards and commendations: credits on a shipped video for Nintendo Wii, Director of Animation for a feature film, an Android application ("app") developer, and art purchased by the Red Cloud Museum for their permanent collection. Sheyahshe has represented his culture well by being a Gates Millennium Scholar and a Ronald E. McNair Scholar.

Sheyahshe currently resides near the Oklahoma City metro area with his wife and children. He continues his research, varied interests, and technological innovations, always keeping an eye towards Indigenous representation in pop culture.

Virginia Stroud
(b. 1951)

Virginia Alice Stroud graduated from Muskogee Central High School in 1969. She pursued Art and Elementary Education. She attended Bacone Junior College from 1969-1970 then transferred to University of Oklahoma from 1971-73. However, she never completed college. Originally, Stroud wanted to become an Art teacher to secondary or primary schools; due to her astonishing paintings, Dr. Richard West of Oklahoma convinced her to make painting a career. From then, Stroud decided to be a painter for living.

A Cherokee-Muscogee Creek painter, writer, illustrator, orator, and second-generation modernist Native American woman, Stroud's artwork is in many Oklahoma museums. Her artistic illustration of painting and writing children's books focuses on Native American culture, history, heritage, and identity.

Her children's books include *Doesn't Fall off His Horse* (1994), *A Walk to the Great Mystery* (1995), *The Path of the Quiet Elk: A Native American Alphabet Book* (1996), and *The Story of the Milky Way* (1995). Her paintings include *Indianische Kunst im 20 Jahrhundet* (2003), *Montana Spring, Peaceful Interlude, Autumn Secrets, River Walk, High Point, Pleasures of the Heart, Water's Edge, Chilies-Southwest Delight, Song Continues, Before Battle, Afternoon Ride, Quiet Moments,* and *Navajo Three.*

Her purpose of being an orator, children's book writer, and painter is to share Native Americans' oldest traditions to others, as she perceives it is a survival way for the Native American culture. For example, Native American women had certain roles such as caretaker, gatherer, nurturer, and spiritual instructor; therefore, their identification is recognized by their duties and clothing.

She has received various awards for her painting: the Woodlands division of the 2nd Annual American Indian Arts Exhibition (for first place), the 30th American Indian National Exhibition (for first place), Heritage Award, Heard Museum Award (for graphics), artist of the year, and Woody Crumbo memorial (for Best of Show, Best Painting, and Best in the Traditional Category).

In addition, she was honored as Miss Cherokee Tribal Princess (1969-70), Miss National Congress of American Indians (1970-71), and Miss Indian American (1971). Virginia's artworks, children's books, and service as Board of Directors of the Indian Arts and Crafts Association has truly shown her dedication towards the Native American tradition.

Susan Supernaw

Susan Supernaw grew up in a home affected by poverty, domestic violence, and alcoholism. Her means of escape was that she sought refuge in her school activities, dance and her Native American church.

Supernaw's *Muscogee Daughter: My Sojourn to the Miss America Pageant* covers her life in eastern Oklahoma (1950 to 1971).

The Muscogee Creek and Munsee author traces her childhood years in poverty, alcoholism and domestic abuse to her extra-curricular activities and scholastic achievements in school. A cheerleader with a straight A average, Supernaw became a Presidential scholar, earned a Washington, D.C. internship with House Majority Leader Carl Albert, won a National Merit scholarship to college, and was crowned Miss Oklahoma in 1971.

Although she did not win the crown for Miss America, her performance in the competition called very prominent attention to the lives of Native American people living the paradox of being marginalized by history and politics as strangers in their homelands.

In Muscogee Daughter: My Sojourn to the Miss America Pageant, Supernaw tells the story of her journey as a Native American discovering her native heritage while being continually distracted by American life. The story is also about finding strength within and being able to push through, or make it through the hardships. It also is about knowing and accepting help when you need it.

Supernaw's book won the 2003 First Book Award for Prose from the Native Writers' Circle of the Americas under the title *The Power of a Name*.

She is president and owner of BearHawk, Inc., a firm which provides computer consulting, networking, programming, database development, computer-based learning, and web design.

She currently resides in Albuquerque, New Mexico, attends book signings, and recently was a guest speaker with Walter Echo-Hawk at the Tulsa Library where they shared their experiences growing up Native American.

Tim Tingle
(b. 1948)

Tim Tingle is an Oklahoma Choctaw and an accomplished performing storyteller, public speaker, and author. His great-grandfather, John Carnes, walked the Trail of Tears in 1835, and it is this rich history that fuels Tingle's passion for storytelling. As a Choctaw, he aims to share the little-known narratives his Choctaw elders passed onto him with modern Indians, and encourages Native Americans to seek out literature that celebrates the Native American spirit. His dedication to the history of Native Americans and his oral performance background gives his writing a rich cultural background and a natural rhythm.

Tingle earned his Master of Arts degree at the University of Oklahoma. He has guest lectured on college campuses all over the country and also served as a writing instructor at the University of Oklahoma (1998-1999). He has also been featured speaker at the Native American wing of the Smithsonian Institute in 2006 and 2007.

His books include *Texas Ghost Stories: Fifty Favorites for the Telling* (2004), *Spooky Texas Tales* (2005), *Spooky Texas Tales II* (2010), *Spirits Dark and Light: Supernatural Stories of the Five Civilized Nations* (2006), *Crossing Bok Chitto* (2006), *When Turtle Grew Feathers* (2007), *Saltypie* (2010), and *Walking the Choctaw Road* (2003). He has been writing his first adult novel, *House of Purple Cedar*, for twelve years, and it will be released by Cinco Puntos Press in the fall of 2012. House of Purple Cedar is a fictional novel based on events surrounding the arson of Indian girls boarding school in Skullyville, near Spiro, Oklahoma, in 1897.

He has also contributed short stories and articles to numerous publications, some of which are, "Archie's War" (2003) and "Josiah Wilbarger" (2006) in *World Magazine*, "The Choctaw Way" (2005) in *Oklahoma Today*, and "Six Dead Cabbies" (2010) in *Lonestar Noire*. Tingle's artistic contributions also extend to the stage, with his full-length theater piece, "Rolling Back the Rock," a story based on a nineteen year old Choctaw, Clarence Carnes, who was the youngest inmate ever sentenced to Alcatraz Federal Prison, and is Tingle's most requested solo performance.

Tingle has received many professional honors, some of which include the Oracle Award (2003), Talking Leaves Award (2009) both presented by the National Storytelling Network. His book *Crossing Bok Chitto* won the Editor's Choice for the New York Times Book Review in 2006, the Oklahoma Book Award for Best Children's Book in 2006, and the 2008 American Indian Young Literature Award from the American Library Association. *Walking the Choctaw Road* was the Oklahoma Reads Oklahoma Book of the Year in 2005, while *Saltypie* is an Oklahoma Book Award Finalist, and a Notable Book for Global Society, 2011, for the International Reading Association.

Tingle's career as a storyteller and author continues to flourish, as audiences all over the nation enjoy his lively performances and historically rich narratives.

Robert Allen Warrior
(b. 1963)

Born in Marion County Kansas, Robert Allen Warrior (Osage) never planned on having a lasting career as an educator, but has lived the majority of his life teaching. He has spent his life as both an author and scholar and contributed his knowledge and works in a vast field of study centered primarily on Native American history, especially their literature, social movements and culture.

He began his education at Pepperdine University where he graduated sigma cum laude with a B.A. in Speech Communication. He went on to earn his M.A. from Yale in Religion and also a Ph.D. from Union Theological Seminary in Systemic Theology. He has held many positions in his academic career. In 1995 he served as an advisory board member for Academic Systems, Inc. developing a multimedia writing curriculum. In 1999 he held a post as a visiting professor at Cornell University where he taught English and American Indian Literature. In 2000 he moved to Norman, Oklahoma, and joined the faculty at the University of Oklahoma. He is now the Director of American Indian Studies at the University of Illinois at Urbana-Champaign. He is also the founding President of Native American and Indigenous Studies Association (NAISA).

His most notable literary contributions include *Tribal Secrets: Recovering American Indian Intellectual Traditions* published in 1995 by the University of Minnesota Press, *Like a Hurricane: The Indian Movement from Alcatraz to Wounded Knee* (with Paul Chaat Smith) published in 1996 by the New York Press, and *The People and the Word: Reading Native Nonfiction* (co-authored with Craig Womack and Jace Weaver) published in 2006 by the University of Minnesota Press. Warrior also served as the New York correspondent for the *Lakota Times* and has had an assortment of publications in a variety of magazines including: *American Quarterly, Genre, World, Literature Today, News from Indian Country*, and *Village Voice*.

He has also had an affiliation with the film world. Warrior has worked in New York with the Children's Television Workshop, appeared in James Fortier's documentary *Alcatraz is Not an Island*,

and also participated on and off screen for The History Channel. In 2009 he worked with PBS as an Academic Advisor for the mini series *We Shall Remain* which focused on key events of Native American history.

Awards and recognition for his literary works include First Place Award for a General Media Article from the Native American Journalists Association (1992), the Deans Fellowship for Junior Faculty from Stanford University (1995-1996), and he also received the prestigious Beatrice Medicine Award for Scholarship in American Indian Studies (2007). He has traveled the U.S. as well as outside the country to France, Malaysia, Guatemala, and Mexico giving lectures in a variety of universities.

Warrior has adopted a style of writing that is different from that of other Native American authors, but he still manages to convey the same sense of traditions and tribal pride. Rather than placing a great deal of emphasis on the ancestral side of Native American Literature he focuses on what being "Indian" means to those of our generation. He believes that by understanding the modern social realities of a Native American in today's society it will bring a better understanding of the past. He remains an involved member with the Osage nation and is especially concerned with the preservation of their language and the I-LON-SCHKA Dance.

Mary Jo Watson

Dr. Mary Jo Watson (Seminole) is a very versatile professional. Aside from serving as Curator for many art programs, including the first Seminole Fine Arts exhibit and two traveling art exhibitions, Watson has also been a member of several committees. Currently, she is a board member for Red Earth and the Jacobson Foundation, a member of the content committee for the Oklahoma History Center, and part of the Seminole Tribal Arts Council.

She is not only the Curator of the prestigious Fred Jones Jr. Museum of Art at the University of Oklahoma, but she also works as the director of the university's School of Art and Art History and as a professor of art and art history. She also developed several courses at her Alma Mater, the University of Oklahoma, including undergraduate classes ranging from an introductory geoscience course to several 20th and 21st century art courses. She also developed graduate classes which include diverse 20th and 21st century art courses as well.

For all of these achievements and more, Watson has received many honors in the past twenty years. Some of these achievements include the Governor's Arts Award for significant contribution to enhance the arts in Oklahoma in 1993, College of Fine Arts Outstanding Faculty Award in 1997, Special Recognition for Outstanding Service by Native American Women in 2003, and most recently Paseo Art Association's Lifetime Achievement Award in 2010.

For over twenty years, Watson has been an enormous part of the art program at the University of Oklahoma. From teaching to course development, from curating to creating the first art history doctoral program in Oklahoma, Watson has proved her worth not only to the university's past but also to the history of Oklahoma. Her advocacy and enthusiasm for the understanding of Native American arts and traditions resounds throughout her career and will continue to do so for many more years to come.

Daniel H. Wilson
(b. 1978)

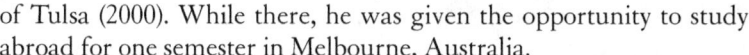

Daniel H. Wilson (Cherokee) was born in Tulsa, Oklahoma. His father was a mechanic and owned his own shop, while his mother worked as a nurse at a local hospital. Since he was a little kid, Daniel found a passion in mechanics and has always had many questions and curiosities about how things worked.

With respect to his education, Wilson graduated from Booker T. Washington High School (1996). He earned a Bachelor's in Computer Science from the University of Tulsa (2000). While there, he was given the opportunity to study abroad for one semester in Melbourne, Australia.

His passion for school and hunger for knowledge of machinery led him to attend one of the top academic institutions in the world, Carnegie Mellon University. While at Carnegie Mellon, he obtained a Master of Science in both Machine Learning and Robotics as well as a Ph.D. in Robotics.

After receiving his doctorate, Wilson hosted the History Channel television series *The Works* (2008). The show examined the origin, usage, and disposal of everyday items such as guns, sneakers, garbage, beer, robots, skydiving, garbage, power tools, motorcycles, steel, and tattoos.

With regard to publications, his early works include *How To Survive a Robot Uprising: Tips on Defending Yourself Against the Coming Rebellion* (2005), *Where's My Jetpack?: A Guide to the Amazing Science Fiction Future That Never Arrived* (2007), *How To Build a Robot Army: Tips on Defending Planet Earth Against Aliens, Ninjas, and Zombies* (2008), and *The Mad Scientist Hall of Fame* (2008). His recent works include *Bro-Jitsu: The Martial Art of Sibling Smackdown* (2010), *A Boy and His Bot* (2011), and *Robopocalypse* (2011).

In such a brief amount of time, Wilson has progressed from budding engineer, scientist, and writer to *New York Times* Bestselling Author. Likewise, he has enhanced significantly the public's understanding of science, technology, and robotics.

Craig S. Womack
(b. 1960)

Craig S. Womack (Muscogee Creek and Cherokee) is an associate professor of English at Emory University in Atlanta, Georgia. At South Dakota State University, Womack earned a M.A. in English (1991). Later, Womack would graduate from the University of Oklahoma with a Ph.D. in English (1995). Womack is a scholar of Native American studies and of gay, lesbian, transgender studies.

He has organized events at Emory University such as "Cosmopolitan and (Trans) Nationalism" and "Native and Latina (o) Interventions." He has also given speeches at the Emory University that include "The Survival of the Mvskoke Creek Language" (2010) and "The History of Mvskoke Creek Government" (2011).

His books include *Red on Red: Native American Literary Separatism* (1999), *Drowning in Fire* (2001), *American Indian Literary Nationalism* (2006), *Reasoning Together: The Native Critics Collective* (2008), and his most recent *Art as Performance, Story as Criticism: Reflections on Native Literary Aesthetics* (2009). His short stories include "Dancing Around the Fire" (1993), "Speaking into the Dawn" (1993), "Lucy, Oklahoma, 1911" (1993), "The Witches of Eufala Oklahoma" (1994), and "Hici" (2000). His poetry includes "Two Men Laughing at the Dawn" (1994), "Quilting" (1995), and "Apparitions" (1995). His most recent works include a manuscript *Hearing Losses and Gains*, "The King of the Tie Snakes"(2011), "The Spirit of Independence"(2011), "There is No Respectful Way to Kill an Animal"(Spring 2012), and "Tribally Specific Literature and Public Scholarship"(Summer 2012).

Womack has also written numerous book reviews, articles, and papers. His articles include "The Academic Habit: A Unique Co-curricular-based Honors Course" (1993), "Alexander Posey's Nature Journals: A Further Argument for Tribally" (2001), "Thomas E. Moore's Sour Sofkee in the Tradition of Muskogee Dialect Writers" (2006), and "Tribal Paradise Lost but Where Did I Go? Native Absence in Toni Morrison's *Paradise*" (2009). Some of his essays include "National Literatures: Making a Return to Native

Communities" (1995), "Native American Literature: A Forward-Looking Conversation" (2000), and "Intersections of Native Studies and Queer Studies" (2003).

He is a member of the Woodcraft Circle of Native Writers and Storytellers National Caucus. In 1997, he received the Woodcraft Circle Storyteller of the Year award for readings and performance. In 2000, he received the award for Woodcraft Circle Writer of the Year in the category personal and critical essays for his book *Red on Red: Native American Literary Separatism*.

FICTION

Mark A. Bowers

Guesswork

A man awoke to find his world transformed. Or perhaps *transformed* is not the appropriate word. It's difficult to describe, words being as they are, mere guttural groans and intonations that like water take on the varied forms and shapes of whatever neuro-pathways they happen to inhabit, the realization of this fluid, linguistic relativity being one of the many not-yet-grasped catalysts behind his sudden change in worldly perspective. The other reasons being so numerous, varied and minute that years of analytical study could never isolate and name them all, like an endless string of firecrackers viewed from a molecular level, the ignition of billions upon billions of microscopic compounds in a chain reaction impossible to predict or follow. And yet, as fruitless an endeavor as he believed it to be, he struggled to find the appropriate terminology, if only as an attempt to order his own thinking.

The actual forms of his world had remained intact and this is precisely what vexed him about the word *transformed*. This change was on a more metaphysical plain than substantive. Even names escaped unscathed. A tree was still referred to as a tree and continued to look like a tree but its definition had somehow changed, its purpose redefined, sharpened, blurred. A spoon was still referred to as a spoon and continued to look like a spoon, yet as he utilized one to unload heaps of oatmeal into his equally obscure mouth it was new and strange to him and imbued with a mystery so foreign and full of limitless possibility that he began to grow fearful. He was lost in this new world. Freer, perhaps, but lost and frightened.

He turned twenty-five that day, and to view the world that once seemed so familiar and predictable as utterly new and undefined was quite overwhelming for him. He wasn't sure what to do next and, at the same time, couldn't be certain how much, if at all, any decision really mattered. It was this unshakeable ambiguity that left him paralyzed, unable to search out the answers to menial questions such as what to do with one's day, as he was unable to determine with what gusto such questions should be pursued. Certainly this was a temporary glitch, a glitch that given time would work itself out with the eventual outcome of purposeful and unencumbered motion. Yes, time is what would be required. Presently though, he was thankful that most of his day had been preordained by his sister—a noon gathering of family in honor of his twenty-fifth. Until then, he would attempt to go about his Saturday as normal—just the normal routine—but with *new eyes in a new world* in a new year. When he thought of this, he discovered that even routine was suddenly plagued with uncertainty. Uneasy though he was, he pushed forward determinedly.

Picking up the morning paper, he sat down to peruse the editorials. The words danced about him like music, full of motion but with more dissidence than harmony. He became lost in the palpitating rhythms, the innumerable competing voices—some crooning, some screeching, others wielding their incongruent melodies like hatchets—the disconnected bridges, the unfamiliar melodies wholly unfollowable, the nonsensical lyrics as well as those offering such varied and contradictory meaning that they forfeit meaning altogether—all this combined about his head in a heavy Play Dough gray mass that seemed to seep into every orifice—his ears, eyes, nose, throat—until at last he could no longer breathe. He finally let the paper fall to the floor and took a gasping breath like the one he took as a youth after fighting off the east coast undertow to resurface strained and discombobulated, stumbling to the shore to collapse in the warm, yellow, Cape Hatteras sand, a gash marking his forehead, having dragged the bottom. No one had seen his struggle or was even aware. Thirty yards down shore his family sat on beach towels under striped umbrellas, eating oranges and drinking lemonade. Meanwhile, he had not only faced death but relived his own choking, violent, watery birth. It seemed to him that these types of struggles were almost always made in private, absent of witnesses.

He left the paper on the floor and headed out the door in the direction of the park, walking past a sluggish lizard slowly breaking free of its winter skin beneath a small, ragged cedar near his front door. As he walked, he attempted to reel in his thoughts but the more he reeled the wirier and more cumbersome the spool became until it finally uncoiled pell-mell within the bony confines of his skull. At this point, in desperation, he took the opposite approach and hastily began to cast the wiry threads out of his head behind him.

The park was a fountain of life and color, spring having reached its undeniable crescendo. Brightly clothed children freed of their winter garb and armor darted across the path before him and about his sides. Dogwoods, their branches heavy with the chatter of birds, blossomed in white and pink. The lavender glow of redbuds dotted the undergrowth of forest that lay ahead. The groupings of parents attending to the frenzied minions of children nodded and saluted his form as he passed and then quickly thought ill of him for his repeated and awkward lack of response. They were not aware of the many tendrilled masses of draglines leeching from his head onto the chat-padded trail behind him, the vibrant forms about him being but a blur of passing clouds and phantoms drawn into his mind and then cast behind. He was not quite insane, but merely on the verge, or a verge of something—good, bad, or spade-gray neutral; he did not know.

He reached a point, after being swallowed within the forest alone, when the voices of children and machines were allayed nearly to oblivion by the woody towers about him, that the spiraling lines behind met a snag and tensed until his movement was halted altogether. Another step and he felt as if his brain would tear and slip from his head like a fetus from an encroaching womb. He left the trail, completely lost from view, and sat down and wept, his back to an old gnarled oak. He felt the undertow once more and for a moment entertained the thought of surrender but staunchly pushed it aside.

When he was born he entered the world a month or so early, silent and as blue as a Smurf. He hung from his mother's weeping vagina with an umbilical noose tight about his neck, gasping to breathe but failing. He was quickly cut free and carted off to ICU while the doctor stayed behind to sew up the jagged exit wound he had created. He spent the next month in the hospital learning to breathe. Some said he had fought for his life while his mother adamantly maintained his survival had been solely the result of a miracle. To that day his mother would often cup his cheek and refer to him affectionately as her *little miracle*, or *God's little gift*. He began to question his mother's claims the day he almost drowned. There was no miracle to speak of that day, only muscle, adrenaline and the relentless tug and gush of water—water heaved and tossed by thoughtless winds and pulled through currents by the clocklike rotation of the planet—waters that receded and retreated by the command of a lifeless rock some 240,000 miles from the spinning earth. Did the earth's rotation stop momentarily that day and halt its relentless currents? Did the moon change course and adjust the daily tides? Did the seas part? There was no miracle anywhere within the vicinity of that warm, yellow beach. No, he had fought for his life with every ounce of muscle that clung to his skinny body and had the skinned knuckles and bloody forehead to show for it. And so it was with every other accomplishment and milestone in his life, so why not his birth? He entertained this thought the day of his near-drowning but only managed to accept it twenty-five years after he had ripped through his mother to enter the world.

On his return, he was a bit more aware of his surroundings. Not aware enough to warrant the descriptor *in tune with nature* but enough to allow him to at least acknowledge the groups of parents he passed along the way and to proffer proper, although rather timid, greetings as he passed. Some nodded warily in reply. Others chided themselves for perhaps misjudging him previously. Still, others were not quite certain they had even seen him before, looking so different as he did without the weight of a hundred thousand draglines pulling at the back of his skull. He may or may not have even whistled a nameless tune on the way back to his apartment.

"The only day that boy's ever been early was the day he was born," bitched one crusty uncle or another just as he fumbled through the front door.

Through curtains of warm, jovial laughter, his mother skirted the room to wish him a happy birthday. She kissed his cheek and whispered something vague about a miracle into his burning ear. He cringed beneath the weight of her statement. The room spun for a moment but the comfortable familiarity of the place helped to reign in his confused and racing thoughts.

He seated himself on his sister's overstuffed, linen sofa between an uncle and a cousin and slowly sank into the deep pit of the pillow-back like a caterpillar dumbly entering its pupal stage of life. His eyes glazed and though he stared and stared he saw nothing. He could no longer see but he could feel the warm swirling eddies of family banter rise about him and wash over his paralyzed form.

It was all familiar, the predictable recounting of past events (the time grandpa locked himself out while going for switches, the time one uncle's snake got loose and bit the other uncle in the ass—the other uncle getting switched for screaming repeatedly in the presence of the visiting pastor, *A snake bit my ass! A snake bit my ass!* The time an aunt's freshly permed hair caught fire while smoking with her boyfriend behind the bus barn), the good-natured teasing and that with a subtle bite, the political rants, the menial discussion of jobs, weather, religion, children, school, and so on. And all of this predictable, monotonous ruckus underwritten by the high pitch, high volume screech of the children at play. He sat and listened to the drone in silence, unable to join in for the disorganized and frantic clutter of his mind.

Then, one uncle asked him a question. "Well?" the uncle repeated, a little put out.

His paralytic lips pursed to form words that would not come while his eyes strained to communicate his dilemma. His tongue was bound by silken threads as were his limbs. He seemed shackled within a dream, unable to move, unable to speak.

"You okay there, boy?"

Suddenly his grandfather rose to say grace, the report from the kitchen being that lunch was officially ready. The uncle finally gave up on receiving a reply and solemnly bowed his head in preparation for the prayer.

The prayer was concise and carefully worded. An invisible deity was addressed as Father and then thanked for its love, grace and the *blessed gift* of birth. It was also thanked for sending its son to earth for the purpose of letting him die. Finally, a special blessing was asked to fall upon the food that it might nourish the body.

Much, if not most, of this prayer he now thought strange. He wondered what was meant by *blessed* food and he wondered if his grandfather even knew? Did some present believe that as the result of this prayer the deviled eggs and potato salad would miraculously morph into the two thousand year old, stale flesh of a dead man? It would certainly be dust by now. Or did some believe that the cake and ice cream would be touched and transformed by this blessing so that upon ingestion it would break down into substances that would *nourish* the body rather than harm it? And how could this deity be thanked for letting its son die when just moments before the gift of birth and life had been lauded? It was curious that he had never made these observations before. But what struck him most were the references to love and grace. These words beat against his ensnaring, stodgy cocoon with enough force to create a small tear and then clung to it like dryer socks to synthetic fabric. He was unsure how these terms could be applied to an entity that had never been seen much less heard from. He could no longer make this leap and did not see the need to when the agents of grace and love that existed within his life were seated and standing about him. Why look elsewhere when what he had been seeking was before him? This fact seemed like solid ground, and so he rose to his feet and thanked his gracious hosts before indulging upon the food prepared and blessed for him by the thoughtful hands of his sister.

Later that afternoon, as he made his way back to his apartment, he marveled at the blueness of the sky and the fresh clarity of air about him, and so once more did not notice the lizard that dwelled beneath the small cedar by his front door. Freed of its winter skin, it now feasted upon it... reborn. Yes, *reborn*, that sounds about right.

Matthew Vasiliauskas

The Contest of Floating Light

In Dodge, the hole was the only attraction.

For decades, the eyes of time viewed the town as a resting hand, its long, slender hills like fingers tightly bound underneath an endless plain of green, shivering grass, held in place by the painful, petrified roots of trees stretching deep within the soil; an inverted, crumbling sky of frozen lightning.

It had remained like this for many years, until one day the angry grip of wind had latched itself onto the nail of one of the fingers, pulling with all its strength, bending it back, centipedes and crickets hopping from the falling, disintegrating orbs of dirt, the cracking of branches and rocks screaming into the fluttering wings of frightened birds, until finally discarding the severed ground into the current of passing wind, leaving only the hole to take in its first gasping breaths.

As far as anyone could tell, there was no bottom to it, and the townspeople took to throwing any random object they could find into the darkness of its throat, kneeling down and allowing their ears to peer over the edges awaiting the distant crash of a vase or water pitcher as it smashed and shattered along the cold ground. But there was only silence.

Young boys would walk up to it, their calloused feet scratching the irritated dirt, and would pull down their pants and begin to piss into it, a dehydrated rippling steaming stream of golden waste falling for miles until finally landing in a pool of swirling, pungent liquid holding schools of blind anxious fish, their eyes born to feel and see only the silkiness of melting white, and their hearts and frayed tails moving in sync, searching desperately for a source of warmth that never comes.

Every August was the contest of light, where a handful of the town's strongest young men would attach two small lanterns to their waist and using a series of ropes that had been set up, swing over the hole, performing various acrobatic stunts against the night sky.

There was always the element of danger, with usually at least one of the contestants losing their grip on the rope, and plummeting into the hole, their screams fading quickly into the hungry darkness.

Hundreds would pour into Dodge for the event, transported in the squeaking, green torn seats of rusted buses, curious faces pressing their nose and eyes into the water-stained glass of the windows, making out broken, faded blurs of passing homes and neighboring cars, young women gripping onto steering wheels, their low-cut dresses revealing a landscape of moist summer flesh and their faces a distorted mesh of shadow and rolling ground.

For this year's contest, all eyes seemed to be on Ruin Parr. His father and brother had won it in the past, and expectations were high for Ruin to carry on the tradition.

He had been training with his father as long as he could remember, waking up as the loose ribbons of dawn wrapped around the gathered clouds of morning, swinging over the lake behind their house, watching apparitions of himself tumble and flip through the murky mirror of the water.

Rarely was there a moment he could escape these sessions, and often would be awoken in the middle of the night by his father bursting into his room, kneeling beside his bed, holding a lighter up to his face, the orange glow spilling into the wrinkles and scars asking Ruin to hit him, screaming it, until the flame seemed to scurry away, sprinting in sheer panic over the loose, scattered clothes until finally escaping through the open doorway where his brother stood, a human-shaped hole leaning against the chipped, wooden paneling, consuming the echoes of exploding saliva.

It was a record crowd for the contest, with most being forced to sit some distance away from the hole. A strong evening breeze made the scene transform into a field of paper grass, cutout, glossy magazine dolls flapping like a million tiny handmade flags.

Ruin along with the five other contestants began to stretch as the judges inspected their lanterns and harnesses. He suddenly felt a tingling sensation shoot through his body, making it hard to swallow, and leading him to try and remedy the situation by discretely gripping onto a small patch of flesh near his hip and pinching it intermittently for what must have been several minutes.

Finally, after a brief speech by the mayor, the contest was ready to begin, with the contestants lining up single file awaiting their turn.

It first began with the palm of a hand, crisscrossing dirty lines of language learned from the warmness of the womb, wrapping tightly around the layers of brown fiber that clung to the magnetized white and pink of the skin.

Soon the lights emerged, swinging back and forth, humming and clanging against the legs and sides of the contestants as they rose and fell, their eyes blinking frequently, and their bodies changing shape as if they were clay, invisible hands molding them into abstract swirling balletic figures propelled by the nervous breaths of the spectators.

One by one they performed their routines, in a constantly shifting world where the stars of night now grazed their bare feet, and the cold surface of the moaning hole spoke painful shivers into the floating tips of their fingers.

It was in this moment that Ruin became an illuminated splash of living water, a new kind of organism, tentacles of light mating with the hanging rope, a cacophonous explosion of rapid breaths and heartbeats swirling in an all-encompassing solar tornado.

As his bare feet hit the ground, tossing up a light haze of lingering dirt, an eruption of applause overtook the area. Hats flew and the glistening from the tear-filled eyes made the field seem like an unending sparkling gem.

A tall, husky man lifted Ruin onto his shoulders, leading the celebratory procession to the awaiting tents holding the food for the reception, as his fellow competitors remained still, defeated statues, their gazes permanently drawn to the ground as if it were the sun, while their lanterns slowly inched back and forth in the breeze.

Children pressed their faces against balloons, as the violin music mixed with the aroma of roasted duck and potatoes. Ruin had been seated near the front of one of the tents so that the townspeople and visitors could shake his hand or touch his shoulder, asking him what did it feel like to float?

All of it was an overpowering buzz to him, stuck in a bright honeycomb, the hairy legs of insects brushing over his face as they flew by, leaving him drenched in the thick sap of his own sweat.

He soon sat up from the chair, brushing past the suffocating crowds until finally emerging from the tent and sprinting back through the field and up to the hole.

His lanterns had dimmed now, their own breaths strained, barely strong enough to moisten the soiled glass.

As he closed his eyes he could hear the voices, unable to rest, dozens of anguished limbs gripping onto the sides of the hole, struggling with every ounce of strength to pull themselves to the surface, but becoming entangled in the grove of ancient roots.

He began to hum, and taking in the scent of distant, burning wood, pinched a small area above his right knee and lept into the darkness.

Diana Campos

IKEA

From under the highway the huge blue building takes over the sky with horizontal block letters more yellow than the sun. Like its own biosphere, the entrance is livened with one—two—three artificial plants. If the walls are its atmosphere, then the looming escalator within is a mountain to climb—if only in simulation.

"Welcome to IKEA—Life changes available." A man's voice, in perfect pitch, resounds from above near the ceiling with all its bright lights. The young couple is interested in changing their lives.

The showroom. The couple is thrust into the land of home improvement. Everything man and woman could possibly use to furnish their home was here, organized into various displays. Displays they could walk into. Displays they could live in—or at least picture themselves living in—for a moment.

First a living room—the EKTORP series—a sofa, armchair, footstool, and chaise each with matching floral cushions. "I'm washable!" reads the yellow sales tag. "Too soft," says the woman. She pokes her husband in his flabby belly in order to move him along. He slaps her face. It stings.

Next a bathroom—the LILLÅNGEN series—modern and compact, with glass mirrors, shelves, soap dispenser, and shower door. "Plenty of organized storage space!" reads the yellow sales tag. "Too fragile," says the man. He shoves his wife with more force than necessary to move her along. She falls on her knees. They bruise.

Then a kitchen—the LYCKHAM series—with solid, white beech surfaces is orbited by six, identical chairs. "Made for everyday life," reads the sales tag. "Too boring," says the man. The man storms off without waiting, leaving his wife behind. She catches up to him and swings her bag around to his face, smashing his nose with the brass buckle. It bleeds.

Finally a bedroom—the MALM series—all square pieces in a birch veneer finish and a thick bed set striped in white and blue. "Fuss-free," read the yellow sales tag. "Too simple," says the woman. The man does not get it. His wife punches him in the groin. He understands.

The couple snatches a quick break to refuel with coffee from the cafeteria. IKEA shoppers stare at them hungrily over their meatballs and salads. Eating. Doing nothing. Bitter and steaming, quite like the hot dark liquid in the ÄLMHULT mugs held by their bruised hands, the couple is quite ready to leave behind the cut-out, windowless rooms.

The market hall. It is a stuffy, underground labyrinth that requires a cart and a map to get through. A right and then a left and then another right. Stainless pots and pans and silverware. Storage boxes, baskets, and jars. A left and then a right and then another left. Bath towels, curtains, and mirrors. Patterned sheets, pillows, and rugs. Another right. Another left. Potted plants, rows of lamps, and mouth-blown vases made of glass. Soon enough their cart is filled with many things. Things they do not really want. They turn the last corner leading out of the maze.

The warehouse. Stacks and stacks of disassembled furniture packed tightly into neat boxes. Boxes full of enough plywood for Noah to build an ark. Were Jesus to be crucified today, perhaps his crucifix would be assembled here.

The couple passes all of this and heads to the lair in which trades are made. It only takes a chunk of their life-savings for home delivery, assembly, and installation services to be arranged. A return policy sign at the exit exclaims: "It's okay to change your mind!"

The couple's house. Old furniture from last month is tossed out, thrown aside by the men in yellow and blue. The new furniture arrives, is assembled, and then placed inside. But it is not enough. All is still again and absolutely no one comes to compliment.

So the couple moves the furniture outside. An entire living room now covers the small lawn in front of their brick living space. There on the grass and dirt are bookcases full of glass vases— empty vases full of nothing. A round oak table and chairs block the sidewalk leading up to their door. On it sits a too-many-piece set of dinnerware and a plastic flower centerpiece. The new porcelain tub peers out from behind the trimmed shrubs. Their dramatic queen-sized bed and bulky wardrobe spill over onto the driveway. The neighbors gather around to ogle at the scene.

The couple is proud of the redecoration, until they realize a few pieces have broken. The instructions are pulled out, drawn up so simply but not as easily understood. Light fixtures collapse. Even the rugs start to fray. More pieces begin to crumble and split.

"Too cheap!" sobs the woman.

"Too dim!" screams the man.

The audience laughs.

Hammer to nail. Saw to board. Peg into hole. Everything falls apart in their hands. The upholstery on the couch tears, the coffee table loses a leg, and the bed is thrown out, not to be used for lack of a mattress. The perfect home has divorced the young couple and the neighbors have all seen. The couple is left with no choice. The furniture must be fixed.

The man shoves a light bulb into the woman's mouth and yanks on her hair.

The woman tears off the man's limbs and replaces them with pegs.

The man sands down his back on the gravel then flips upright, onto all four wooden legs.

The woman drives her toe nails into the concrete walkway.

Their blood, thick like lingonberry jam, stains the carpet-strewn lawn red. A thunder cloud rolls menacingly overhead, thick and dark gray. The audience begins to disperse before the cloud can burst open on the human furniture and try to wash the display away.

And inside, the house remains quiet and empty.

Kenneth L. Levine

Checkmate

Outside the rats scream and their claws scratch. I slap my hands together, then drink my Cisco Red while I listen to them scatter.

After the third swallow I'm awake enough to remember the Sunday morning when John's eyes shined brightly with youthful pride as he said "checkmate" for the first time and I tilted my king on its side to acknowledge his victory. John, who was twelve and had been playing chess with me every Sunday morning for five years, ran from the den to the kitchen into the open arms of his mother, exclaiming, "Mom, I did it! I won! I beat dad!" Alice fried eggs, buttered toast, and poured orange juice and coffee and we ate a celebratory breakfast. When John bolted to his friend to report his win, Alice thanked me. I almost told her I didn't lose on purpose as she had been requesting but I realized I was responsible for his victory because I had taught him how to play chess. We kissed, went to our bedroom and made love.

I take another three gulps and with my eyes closed I can picture my Alice as she leaned over me with her breasts clapping and her strawberry locks tickling my nose. It's an incomplete image. I can't focus. I can't feel her. She's gone.

I squat, lift up the flap cut into one of the long sides of the corrugated, cardboard box that was previously the packaging for a Kenmore refrigerator and crawl into the alcove beneath Houston Street. Clasping a brown paper bag in my left hand and a stick to ward off rats in my right, I walk slowly through the stifling heat, grateful for a 600 foot train that fans the subterranean air as it roars past. I walk two blocks in the dark with a wall of the tunnel to my right while swatting rodents and being careful to avoid stepping on other mole people and the remnants of their crack pipes, empty wine bottles and hypodermic needles.

When I reach the stairs that lead to the platform of the subway I drop the stick, climb the stairs and exit into the blinding light and traffic of Second Avenue. Trapped in the collective movements of the surface dwellers that underscore the meaninglessness of my life, I maneuver to the side of the street and pause, slide the paper bag down the neck of the bottle inside, undress it, lift its lips to mine and thirstily drink my Cisco Red while I remember that it used to be my Alice whom I lovingly undressed, kissed, drank and craved until she said, "I want you out of here." And I was gone.

I walk to the corner of Houston, turn right and make a left on Broadway. I pass Little Italy and Chinatown to my left, then City Hall to my right. I stop at the corner of Fulton, face right and look skyward where the Twin Towers of the World Trade Center stood before they crumpled and left a gaping hole in my universe. I take another three gulps of my liquid crack while I remember John, Alice and I as we sat in the family room of our house in Queens and watched the planes repeatedly crash into the towers on television. John said, "It's like a fly hitting our home and making it collapse." I said, "A fly isn't filled with fuel."

I walk to the intersection of Broadway and Wall Street and sit on the stoop facing Trinity Church. Perhaps I stop here often because it's a house of God, although God is never home or elsewhere. At least that would explain my life. Maybe it's because the Church is an Episcopal Church and in that way is a house of my father, the Rt. Reverend Joseph Stringer, Bishop, Episcopal Church, Armed Services, a man who, like God, has never been home for me.

I enter the Trinity Churchyard and sit on a bench in its park-like grounds amidst the few graves of well known, interred, historical figures such as Alexander Hamilton, William Bradford, Robert Fulton, Albert Gallatin and Captain James Lawrence and the many graves of others who died between 1697 and the mid 1800's. Except for me it's a cemetery without mourners. They too have died. But grief is everywhere. In the slightest breeze I hear the cries of loved ones who stood graveside in centuries past. The grass must be so green because of all the tears they shed as their loved ones became fertilizer underfoot.

I walk among the dead and read the inscriptions on their tombstones, which rise vertically or lie horizontally on the ground, like fallen soldiers. I fill in the many letters and numbers that time has eroded. Mourners die; monuments fade.

On my right a tombstone reads: "Here Lies the Body of Deborah Wife of John Dowers who departed this Life Oct'r 21, 1761 aged 42 years. Fare well a thousand Times Dear. Till we shall meet & never part." I feel his love for her, the all-consuming vacuum of his loss.

A few steps away the grave is that of Juliet, daughter of Samuel and Catharine Lockman. Only their names and the words, "Parents weep," are still legible. I know they weep. They weep and try to forget but they can't. And they die inside because nothing challenges the order of the universe more than the untimely death of a child.

On the tombstone next to Juliet's the inscription reads: "Here Lie the bodies of two infant brothers. Valentine Morris Wilkins and Isaac Wilkins. The first departed this Life on the 24th September 1793, aged 1 year and 5 days, the second on the 1st Feb. 1794, aged 5 years and 2 months. We were born to die: Tis but expanding thought and life is nothing." I despise those words. Children are born to live! Their life is everything. Without them there is nothing. Nothing!

I down more of my Cisco Red and remember that when I pressed my ear against Alice's bare, bulging belly to listen to John kick, Alice stroked my hair and said, "I've been researching names and think we should call him 'An.'"

I sat up. "In Vietnamese that means peace, peacefulness."

Alice smiled. "I know. Isn't it a beautiful name?"

I shook my head. "I want him to be Americanized. It will be easier for him to be successful if he has an American name. Let's name him John."

Alice frowned. "I think we should instill in him a sense of his past. I want him to be proud of his Vietnamese heritage. I think we should give him a Vietnamese name."

I said, "You haven't experienced bigotry. Believe me, when you have Caucasian and Asian blood, it isn't possible to forget your Asian roots."

What if I had named him An instead of John? What if I hadn't taught him how to play chess? Chess is descended from a game originated in India in the 6th century called Chaturanga, a Sanskrit word referring to the four divisions of an Indian army—elephant, cavalry, chariots and infantry. Worse still, my handcrafted chess pieces were representative of the Third Great Crusade led by King Richard I of England, who in 1189 joined King Phillip II of France in an effort to recapture the holy city of Jerusalem from the Muslim leader, Saladin. Maybe John joined the army because we played chess, a game depicting war, the Crusades, the Christians against the Muslims, with John always choosing white, the Christian side. Maybe John wouldn't have joined the army to fight Osama Bin Ladin in Iraq if I had named him An.

I tried to stop John from enlisting. I told him about the horrors of the Vietnam War but he was infused with patriotic fervor and wanted to protect America because I taught him that America was noble and good. I had used my life as an immigrant who had come here with almost nothing but still was able to graduate from college and own several markets and a home through my hard work as an example of the wonderful consequences of its nobility and goodness.

A few feet away from the Wilkins' graves, the bond between parent and child is proudly displayed. Samuel Johnson, the father, and Samuel Johnson, the son, were buried thirty-three years apart and lie side by side for eternity beneath their two abutting tombstones.

I counted upon that natural bond and my father's experiences during the Vietnam War the day I flew to Virginia to ask him to convince his grandson not to enlist. Although I grew up believing my father was a United States lieutenant who died in Vietnam during the war, my mother's diary, which I read after she died, revealed he left Vietnam before I was born. Seven years later he sent her what she called "guilt money," which she used to move us from Vietnam to New York City. According to the diary, after a claymore created something like a football field scattered with the arms, legs, entrails and other body parts of the enemy, my father and his men sifted through the pockets of the dead for money and war trophies as if it were Christmas morning. When he found a photo of a dead man and his smiling wife and three girls, he made an excuse and burned the treasures because he felt like he had stolen a piece of their lives. Although my mother was shattered when my father deserted her, I, as a child of war, had felt kinship with him each time I imagined him lighting the fire.

For years I had known where my father lived and that he had become a bishop but I was afraid to confront him. Necessity finally conquered my fear and I stood at my father's door not knowing what to expect.

"I'm your son, Hien Tang," I said when the door opened to reveal the man who had given me his blue eyes and square jaw.

"I have no son," he said.

"My mother was Huong Tang," I said to the man who had given John his blond hair and six-foot height.

"I have no son," he said.

"I read her diary. It said you were her lover, my father."

"I have no son."

"I read about the claymore, how you saw the smiling family photograph of the dead Vietcong soldier. My son, John, your grandson, wants to enlist. I need you to help me convince him not to."

"I have a wife and daughter. You're not my son. I have no grandson," he said before he slammed the door in my face. And he was gone.

The next inscription I read says: "Here Lyes Interred ye Body of Benjamin Thomas who Departed this life Aug. 1, 1744 As you ayer now So once was I In helth & Strength thoe here I lye & as I am now So you must be Prepair for Death & Follow me." I'm too distracted to think about its meaning. Everything itches. Beneath my beard and under my balls and my armpits and in my anus there are millions of tiny pinches and little bites from an army or armies of things crawling and driving me to distraction. I scratch and keep scratching, rubbing myself raw, but it's pointless. I take five more gulps of my Cisco Red. It's the fuel I need to move and I have to walk so that the stepping of my legs and the swinging of my arms distract me.

I trot from the graveyard and walk north on Broadway as I look into each garbage can I pass for food. I see a discarded quarter of a quarter-pounder in a Burger King wrapper, an uneaten apple with teeth marks, some cookies with black bits that look like chocolate chips or raisins but they could be ants that aren't crawling, a couple of pieces of white bread, a discarded bouquet of rotting flowers and the cover of the Daily News.

I read the newspaper's headline:
"ROT IN HELL!
Obama: U.S team kills Bin Laden in firefight"
that partially covers Osama Bin Laden's picture. I run my hand through my beard, which is as long as Bin Laden's, and stare into his eyes. I can discern neither good nor evil. Although I know this is what John wanted, I feel nothing. I eat the burger, apple and bread, but leave behind the cookies because the black bits are ants, while I try to think of a reason why I shouldn't follow Benjamin Thomas.

I toss the Bin Laden cover back in the garbage and remove the bouquet. Carrying the flowers I turn right on Fulton Street and pass a market that reminds me of the three markets I owned before my company failed. It has been easy to dismiss the loss of material things but no matter how much I drink I haven't been able to forget those I've loved and lost. I raise the bottle and swallow hungrily until it's empty. After the last drop of the red syrupy hooch coats my throat and gullet I wait for oblivion but it still isn't enough.

I turn left on Nassau Street and stop at a liquor store where I buy a 375 ml bottle of Cisco Red for $1.99. Outside I pull the neck of the bottle from the bag, open it and drink more Cisco Red, titling my head back until it gushes down my throat and its overflow oozes from my lips and stains my beard and tattered clothes the color of the blood shed by John on June 12, 2005 when he became the 1,706 th United States solder killed in Iraq. According to a letter I received from John's company commander, John's platoon stopped a suspicious van in Baghdad and ordered the man inside to leave the vehicle. The man walked toward John and blew himself and John up.

I remember sitting on the back porch of my house a few months after I was notified of John's death. I was drinking a glass of scotch after having drunk half the bottle on the table beside me. I was thinking they had turned John into nothing more than number 1,706 after

I had taught him about numbers and how to count, add, subtract, multiply, divide and use them in chess to place values on pieces—pawns, 1 point; knights, 3 points; bishops, 3 points; castles, 5 points; queen, 9 points; and the king, 4 points in the endgame—when Alice entered followed by a middle aged man in a lieutenant's uniform.

"A Lieutenant Stevenson is here to see us," Alice said.

"Isn't that wonderful," I said, ignoring her icy stare.

"Mr. And Mrs. Tang, on behalf of the United States government I am here to present to you a survivor's benefit check in the amount of $100,000. We deeply regret the loss of your son," the lieutenant said.

The lieutenant handed me the check and I stared at it in disbelief. "John's life for $100,000? If you gave me a million it wouldn't be enough. There isn't enough money in the world," I said.

"I'm sorry, Mr. Tang."

"You're sorry?" I extended my hand. "Here. Take it back. Give me back my boy."

"I wish we could, Mr. Tang."

I tore the check into little pieces and scattered them in the air. "That's what you did to my John. Leave my house," I yelled.

"I'm sorry, Mr. Tang," the lieutenant said.

Alice escorted the lieutenant from the porch. When she returned she said, "I've had enough. You stink of scotch. You exhale it. You sweat it. Your pores are saturated with it. You get aggressive and obnoxious and then depressed. You piss in our bed. I can't take it anymore. I want a divorce. I want you out of here."

I looked at her and saw John in her forehead and her nose, in the redness that stained her cheeks and in the movement of her hands. In that moment I knew her presence would always underscore John's absence. I left her and my house and all my possessions with only the clothes on my back and the bottle of scotch. As I walked away she said: "You should have listened to me. We should have named him An."

At the end of Nassau Street I enter City Hall Park and sit on a bench from which I look at the Brooklyn Bridge across the street. There's something majestic, beautiful and lonely about the bridge's Gothic, double pointed, arched towers built of limestone, granite and cement, long, sleek, steel cables strung like harpsichords along its sides and expansiveness that links Manhattan to Brooklyn Heights over the East River. But to me, today, it isn't a bridge to a place; it's a bridge to John. Today I will heed the inscription on Benjamin Thomas' tombstone. I disassemble the bouquet, craft its daisies, lilies, roses, lilacs and freesias into a crown that I place on my head, finish drinking my Cisco Red and toss the bottle in a garbage can.

I cross the street to Park Row and Centre Street and enter the bridge's pedestrian walkway. As I walk toward Brooklyn Heights, swaying slightly from side to side as the bridge oscillates to the steps of the many people around me, I listen to the cars swoosh by in the automobile lanes beneath the wooden walkway. Everywhere people are walking, running, rollerblading, biking, driving, living but the bridge and I are alone with each other.

Fortified by the thought of being reunited with John, I use all my strength to climb over the pedestrian gate and up the cables to the top of the bridge's Manhattan tower. Below me the wind whistles through the cables and the East River beckons. I stare into its waters unsure if I can jump. Am I strong enough? Weak enough?

A gathering crowd on the walkway looks at me. I say to the sky, "Each day points to eternity. The fate of all time depends upon a single moment. My John was stolen. Killed. He'll never feel life growing in the belly of the woman he loves or hold his newborn in his arms. What will become of the woman he would have married or all the people whose lives would have been touched by his children or his children's children? The people whose lives would have been touched by him? He was a chess player, a mathematician, a scientist. Think of what he might have created, the questions he might have answered, the people he might have taught. I miss him. I miss him terribly. I can't stop missing him. He was my conscience, my soul, my heart, my everything. There's nothing without him. How can a father live without his son? It's unnatural. It's wrong. Look at what I've become."

The crowd below swells. It yells something that is drowned out by police sirens. In the automobile lanes beneath the walkway cars are stopped too and their drivers and passengers stick their heads out the windows and shout.

I feel the onlookers' collective concern until the sirens stop and I decipher their chant: "Jump! Jump! Go ahead, jump!"

In a voice too soft for them to hear I say, "Don't you see what war does to all of us? John and I will never play chess again. We'll never hug, laugh, cry together, confide in each other, be father and son, friends, best friends. He'll never give Alice and me a daughter in law or grandchildren or great grandchildren. I'll never again know the love of Alice, the touch of her hand, her lips, her breath, her pulse against mine. I never had the love of a father. Look at yourselves. You wait for me to jump. To you death has no meaning. It's just another statistic you hear about on the news. But John wasn't just number 1,706. They were all more than numbers. They were living, breathing beings with a past and with a future that was everyone's. They're missed. Don't you see when you kill a soldier, you kill his family, all families? War is the end of decency, of civilization."

The chant continues and grows louder and more urgent: "Jump! Jump! Go ahead, jump!"

I study the landscape in the distance. Cold, tall, steel shapes look like icicles scraping the sky. As I walk to the edge of the Manhattan tower a news helicopter flies overhead and I imagine the helicopter as a plane hitting each Twin Tower where it once stood. The two icicles melt, leaving nothing behind. I stare at the water below. Am I strong enough? Weak enough?

I say, "I lost my John—three points; I lost my Alice—nine points; I lost my father—three points; I lost my home—five points; I lost my employees—one point each." I tilt towards the East River and whisper "Checkmate," to the water that rushes me.

Thea Swanson

Broken Moon

At 4:00 A.M., two hours before Ellie's alarm clock was set to ring on her 67th birthday, she woke with a start. For the past twenty years she had dreaded her birthday. It wasn't just because she was turning into an old lady—an unbelievable, slow, painful event that she wished on no one. And it wasn't just because she was lonely— she didn't know when it was worse, during the silent evenings, or with her seventh-grade students to whom she taught Adaptation, as she had for the past fifteen years. No, there was more. She was un-happy because September 29th was not only her birthday, but also, this year, 2032, it was the twentieth anniversary of the broken moon.

Ellie lay in bed, definitely not looking out the window, at the distortion in the sky. Instead, she let her eyes rest on the moonlight that barely lit the wall, a wall she kept primer-white, a white that was bright and harsh, a white that could make her forget that the light in the world would never be what it once was.

"Deathdays," she said in the dark, her voice crackling with mucous as if to support her proclamation. It was hard enough for her on any given day to look in the mirror and see faded eyes and lined cheeks because dammit, that is not what she felt like. Old women crocheted Afghans and asked young people for rides to the doctor. She did neither of these things. Even as a teacher, years ago, even at forty, she had danced in the middle-school lobby to the latest music (After all, she'd been a punk rocker way back). And even these days, she still played underground music, was still captivated by ethereal melodies and driving drums, still played the same song over and over on her ring pod when no one else was around, even though she'd be fined—or worse—if she got caught.

But now with her bones as brittle as they were, full of Swiss-cheese holes that early menopause accelerated, her monthly cycle suddenly stopped from the diminished pull of the moon (finally, mythology could stick its tongue out at science), she couldn't dance. She could only bob her head to the beat, at home, feeling antiquated and trapped. Despite the papery skin of her forearm, she knew what it felt like to wreak havoc with one's body, to slam it into a friend for no reason other than the thrill of contact. But that didn't happen any-more to anyone, anywhere—at least, not above ground. Even if Ellie could dance, no one else would, not that way, not out in the open.

The government had tried to shift the blame. "Get real," she had said to Gary in the car, a lifetime ago, to the news on the radio, driving near the coast at Seaside. "Could it *all* be a coincidence?" Some things, no one could deny—the extinction of numerous coastal life, like the geoducks that used to squirt at toddlers who hunkered next to their moms on the mudflats. But other changes, changes to which science couldn't prove a direct correlation, the government attributed to secondary circumstances—the slumping economy, for instance. They said the loss of jobs caused motorists to drive off bridges. They said that slow business caused restaurant owners to close up shop. Storefront after storefront, boarded-up or abandoned, crept by as Gary steered slowly down the coastal shops during the peak of tourist season. Ellie gaped at a stack of plates left on a counter, a clean, white tablecloth halfway in the process of being draped.

"Sweeping it under the carpet only makes it worse. It drives us *crazy*." She had gritted her teeth, clamped onto the hair at her scalp. Gary had glanced her way, then back to the road, unmoved by her outburst, and like so many others, he had that look in his eye. That look that held the simple, indisputable and horrific knowledge. "Gary, don't. You're scaring me."

"Don't you see, El?" He said, a strand of long, thinning hair falling out of his ponytail, veiling his profile so that Ellie pushed it behind his ear. "Unless you believe in something more than this, what's the point?" They were silent the rest of the three-hour drive home.

People *had* given up, and Ellie had seen on that day that Gary had too. When they made it home, he had flopped on the bed, turned on the TV, and watched the feeble attempt from the president, urging us to keep our chins up, that "we have been through darker days..." His voice had trailed off, the realization of the magnitude of the pun, the great sadness that no, this we could not repair, no matter how much hope we could muster. And then the beginning of the end of Gary as he turned on his side and pulled up his knees.

But humans are a resilient bunch. Maybe not as many or as whole as they once were, but resilient. The moon hung on and so have we. There was much to be thankful for, Ellie forced herself to say aloud, in the dark, on her birthday. She was alive. The population was shrinking, but she was alive. The moon was broken, but she had the memories from when it wasn't. She remembered, as she lay in bed, a time when she visited the Strait of Juan de Fuca, on a late spring day when the tides came in strong, when the waves blasted her feet, the cold Pacific waters. Clear waters that shot a chill all the way from her ankles to her heart. Gary hadn't believed her, that she actually felt her heart go cold. He placed his large hand inside the placket of her shirt. "Nope. Just soft warmth, El." And they kissed in the splash.

But so often, when the memory fizzled away, it was replaced with a more recent one. Waters were now stagnant, murky. Death resided there. Beach chairs and surfing were things of the past, like knights, arrowheads, and pennies. Sea Agitators could only stir things up so much, so deep and so often. It was like watching a cooking show, Ellie had thought just last week, gearing up emotionally for her birthday, watching *Bake Sensibly* on her uniscreen in order to distract herself as she aimed it at the wall above the dryer in the laundry room, folding towels. The cook had simply run a whisk through the eggs twice, had hardly combined the flour, salt and baking soda with a quick spooning. He then pulled the previously prepared dish out of the refrigerator, the *real* dish, the one that had *beaten eggs* and *sifted* powders. *That* was what worked. The real deal, not a meal prepared for the screen, not a machine made for the sea.

Ellie flipped over her pillow, her neck sweaty. Propping herself with her elbow, she reached for a glass of water on the nightstand. About to take a sip, she noticed a gnat, paddling and paddling its tiny wings on the surface, attempting to be free of its unexpected predicament. Placing the glass back on the stand, she lay back.

The alarm rang. Ellie had just fallen asleep, so her head felt as if tens of tiny fingers tapped at her skull, forming white dots behind her closed eyes. The thought of calling in sick entered her mind, but she quickly pushed it away; if she let it linger, she would call in and then feel guilty. Anyway, this day of all days, she couldn't call in. It was her job to teach these kids about their wonderful world, sticking closely to the textcompbook, *Forever Adapting!* The story of the moon was covered in two pages. Some students would come to school curious about the days of the whole moon. Parents might have reminisced in bed, been overheard as houses rested in attentive dread. Ellie didn't want to leave the lesson to a substitute who might stutter, or worse.

Star Middle School was tame, as always. Classes were on the larger size, eight to nine kids, but Ellie was used to it, having taught classes as large as thirty, years ago, when kids had an innate energy that had to be quelled, when boys fidgeted and were given medicine.

Now, Ritaladderall was simply given at birth, along with the vitamin K shot, the bath. Later, with vitamins at the breakfast table. Why take chances.

Ellie's classroom was a quiet, orderly place, as were all classrooms. Oh, how Ellie wished she could scold a boy for leaning back in a chair! In those days, there was a burgeoning. You could feel it! The tapping of the pencil on the desk—they couldn't help themselves. The slamming down of the binders as they entered the room. "I'm here!" That's all they were saying. That's what they really meant. "Look at me!" They weren't being rude. They were just being human. Ellie used to repress her giggles. She understood: they loved life. That was all. Things were different now. No more reaching for the stars. A sense of containment, of fear. We broke the moon, so everything else had to be put in order.

Ellie unlocked her classroom, walked inside. There was a time when desks were doodled-on. Poems and paintings her students created used to hang on the wall, sending messages: *You give them much, Ellie. You matter.* Now her room was kept in check. Desks were individual computer pods; a boy couldn't lean back if he tried. No poems. No paintings. Just information. Ellie would view a row of faces across her screen. The students would view hers in return.

In the empty classroom, she climbed in her pod, legs heavy from no sleep, her blood forever low on iron, her body weak. So that she would loom above the students as dictated, she touched the "raise pod" option on the screen. Lately, she had been stopping short of the required height, and today, she dropped it another inch, now down six inches total. She knew she'd be written up if administration should walk in, but she'd been feeling reckless, been feeling like a timer was about to go, that there was something she had to beat. Just three weeks ago, on the first day of school, she had swerved from her normal introduction and, hand shaking, unfolded a page of a poem she had torn from an old book. Paper rattling, she cleared her throat and read to her screen:

```
Dawn Revisited
By Rita Dove

Imagine you wake up
with a second chance: The blue jay
hawks his pretty wares
and the oak still stands, spreading
glorious shade. If you don't look back,

the future never happens.
How good to rise in sunlight,
In the prodigal smell of biscuits—
```

```
Eggs and sausage on the grill.
The whole sky is yours

To write on, blown open
To a blank page. Come on,
Shake a leg! You'll never know
Who's down there, frying those eggs,
If you don't get up and see.
```

She had lifted her eyes to perplexity, mouths agape, eyes wide or narrowed, confused expressions in a row on her screen. She herself was perplexed because she couldn't ask them to make connections, couldn't ask for understanding. Balling the poem tightly in her lap, she had mumbled something about the importance of a balanced breakfast.

Feeling exposed and shaken, Ellie had reverted with gusto to the rest of the lesson planned for that day. *It's an ever-changing world!* She scrambled to touch the screen to open the textcompbook, telling them to touch theirs. *Change is how we got here in the first place. The primordial soup? Evolution? You'll learn about these. We are still evolving! The breaking apart of Panacea, the flooding of Beringia. Yes, Kelsey, is it? Yes, the moon was our fault—I mean, our doing— but look what we have because of it! Peace. Not so long ago, we were killing each other. Not anymore. Sometimes it takes drastic measures. The Declaration of Co-Dependence. As people of the world, we are finally united. The No-War Treaty signed by every country on the globe. That's something. The disassembling of all weapons, all nuclear plants. Yes, Robert, is it? True. There have been renegade factions—especially lately, but there will always be people who for one reason or another are bent on destruction. The New Privacy Act should help keep an eye on things. But peace! This is new territory.*

Gracie, new to the school, had been slumped in her pod, not looking at her screen. It was clear to Ellie that she wouldn't stay at this school for long and would be sent to one of the two new reform schools that were being built. "Pay attention, Gracie. This will be on your unit test." She had said.

But this day, on her birthday, Ellie didn't have it in her to keep them on track. She felt closure coming. Oh, for sure, she had seen the hope fade from Gary's eyes, and finally his body, and, years ago, she had wanted to keep that from happening to her students. Their lives depended on it! But there was a turning in her that she couldn't muster the strength to turn back, and maybe it was because she was tired, or because it was her birthday, but she couldn't stick to the curriculum. There was something at risk, even if she couldn't place it. She dropped her chair another inch.

Lowering her pod all the way, she climbed out.

Around the nine empty pods, she snaked, touching the gray, dull shimmer of brushed metal. Not a mark on any of them. No gum. No stick figures emblazoned with black Sharpies. No stamp to say, "I was here."

Windows were cut high into the wall to let in daylight, but not to distract. Thick walls built to withstand destruction. Ellie placed her hand on the cold, rough surface, withdrew quickly.

They'd be arriving soon. And she had prepared nothing.

She gripped her arms, let out a breath, and ambled back to her pod.

Inside, she brooded, touched the screen. The school broadcasted a non-stop flow of study techniques, of curriculum standards, of organizational methods. But here was something different. A podcast from years ago.

Ellie expected propaganda on this day, the anniversary. Every year, she had been inundated with patriotic images and texts taken from time immemorial, it seemed—from the beginning of Western Civilization, to the founding fathers, to today. But nothing of the moon itself. Not even Armstrong. But here was something different. A grainy video. Closer and closer to a black-surrounded white orb, the target. Usually, only reunion and union were broadcast, strength and determination, co-dependence and perseverance, but never a moon. The moon, like the stumped arm of a vet. One didn't talk in these terms. One discussed the vet's dedication, his honor, not the missing arm, the hand lying in the rubble.

Ellie pressed the volume pad, but there was nothing. *No sound in space.* Dizzy, she brought her hand to her temple. On the screen were fuzzy pixels zooming in. Gray. Craters. Not wanting to go inside those craters, she turned her head, then peeked and touched the pad to exit the podcast, but the image would not leave the screen, no matter what she clicked.

"Well now." Ellie pulled her chin back, as if smacked by a glove. A dual. Yes, a dare. Pick up your sword. Face me! Watch me. This is the truth. This is what she had never seen. The underground had risen.

There it was.

And there she sat in her pod and watched. And she broke through the craters of her mind, and let the memories collide with the images on the screen.

There had been the desire for water, this she remembered. Not the need, but the desire for future expeditions. How perfect! Like the drive-thru espressos she had been enamored with when having moved to the Pacific Northwest from the East Coast. Mochas while in the car. Water while in the spaceship.

This podcast was like an old silent film—mute drama, overacting. Surely that's what she must be viewing—a reenactment—smash after smash, objects hurling toward the orb, and then sudden gray and white, and a flying away.

Multiple countries had been smashing—*oops!*

Surely someone had to know. Was it all about getting it done first? "Oh, they got it done alright," Ellen said, sickened by the image, but somehow at peace enough to rest her arms on her hollow belly, now that she viewed the truth,.

All that mining, that's what it was, during the year following the forming of the NASA Lunar Science Institute. *Join Us!* They said, *We welcome international partnerships!*

Rubidium was to be the new leader in thermoelectricity. Such a campaign there had been! You'd think they had found the fountain of youth!

Students enter her classroom.

Ellie jolted. Blinked.

"Good morning, Gracie." Ellie said from her pod and then slipped out, leaving the footage playing.

"Good morning," Gracie said in a small voice, still not at home in her new school, finding her way toward the back of the room.

"What a day, what a day," Emily said, straightening her back, walking around the room, smiling, arms crossed. At the rear wall, she looked up to the window. "I just realized," she said, putting her hands on her hips, "I've never tried to open these."

All nine students were in the classroom now, somewhat interested in her discovery.

"No bother." She turned around quickly, almost theatrically, surprising the kids. There's more interesting things to talk about today." As she walked around the room, the kids slid into their pods. The screens brought total comfort and quiet, as they had for years.

Ellie hastened to the front of the room, knowing that once they logged in and entered their passwords, they'd see that image that had changed their lives forever.

"Hold on kids." Ellie pinched the scalloped collar of her blouse. "Before you log on, I want to talk with you, face to face." Nine heads stuck out of their pods, eyebrows pinched.

"Why?" Ernest asked, his brown eyes huge in his smallish head.

"I want to talk to *you*, not the screen." Ellie dropped her voice, bracing herself on the edge of her pod. "Step out, please."

The students stepped out, looked at each other, held their forearms protectively. Ernest frowned. Gracie's eyes were glossy and wide.

Ellie scanned the room, searching for the ghost of circle-time space.

"I've got an idea. Help me out, guys." Marching to the center of the room she tried to push one of the metallic pods. "It's working!

Alice, John—you push those pods toward the wall."

"Why?" John asked, rubbing the top of his buzz-cut.

"Just do as I say."

"Abby, Liz. You go that way."

After half the pods were jammed against the wall, dirty lines remained, like markings at a crime scene.

"Let's sit."

Ellie lowered her body. The sour students followed, adjusting their positions to avoid the smears on the floor.

"Today is my birthday," Ellie announced, letting out a sigh. "I thought we could celebrate."

"How?" Ernest demanded.

"By talking about today. The importance of today." Ellie smoothed down her shirt.

"You mean, because of the moon?" Gracie asked in a low voice, revealing her secret. She rocked her knee that stuck up, a thin arm draped around her leg, her fingers twisting her shoelace.

"Yes, Gracie." Ellie's heart pounded hard. "What do you know about it?" Ellie took deep breaths, her anemia affecting her at times like this, times when she needed more oxygen, times when things felt on the brink.

"That we made a mistake." Gracie answered.

"That's not true. The equipment failed." John picked at the rubber on his sneakers.

"The truth is," and Ellie hesitated, but all eyes were on her, so she had to continue, "we went too far." Ellie examined the faces of this generation, ready to soothe, to apply a carefully worded balm.

"What's the big deal?" Ernest asked, his elbows propped on his knees.

"What's the big *deal?*" She blurted out, slapping her legs, not at all reacting as planned. Her fingers stung, especially her ring finger, still bearing her wedding ring. "Just a minute, guys." Ellie sucked in air between her teeth, rubbing the blue worm of a pinched vein that crept from under her ring. She thought of Gary and his reaction to the news she was about to share. He had aged so quickly that year. These kids—their faces were so smooth. She looked at Gracie's knee poking through a hole in her jeans. That hadn't been the fashion for years. Life was going to be hard for her.

She shook the pain in her hand away. "The big deal is that I used to dance with my students in the school halls." She pointed with her chin to the door.

Gracie stopped twisting her shoelace, lit up. "What kind of dancing?"

"Have you ever heard of," Ellie lowered her voice, "moshing?"

"Isn't that illegal?" John asked, his blue eyes computing.

"Yes, but it wasn't always." Ellie stretched out her legs in front of her, crossed them at the ankles. "And it could be fun."

"And this has to do with the moon *how?*" Ernest's lip stuck up on one side.

"We can't dance." John spoke up, his computation complete. "The national creed—"

"And why not?" Ellie rose from the floor. "That's what I really want to know. Why *not.*" She tapped her ring pod. "Listen to this."

Abby shot Alice a look.

A song from Ellie's adolescence came on, from a band whose leader killed himself—maybe a good thing, she had thought recently. It was a song about teens and spirit. A song about denial. It was a song that Ellie had thrown her body around to, a song played when young adults moped about nothing in particular, when now they had all the reason in the world.

Ellie took off her cardigan that she wore over her blouse. She tied it around her waist, took off her shoes.

Standing now and backing away, the kids watched as their old teacher lifted her arms and brought them down, swayed her head from side to side like some old, large mammal. Arms up, legs up, again and again. Abby shook her head at Alice, crossed her arms. John snickered as the teacher twisted, jumped up and down like a deranged rabbit.

"C'mon guys, don't you feel it?" Ellie implored through labored breaths and pain.

Gracie smiled and joined her, jumping as best she could, flapping her arms, puppet-like.

Holding Gracie's hands, sweaty and weak, Ellie shared the song of rebellion, the glory of movement. The pain in her bones subsided. Just like ages ago, this moment alone, this dance of freedom, was all that mattered.

Slowing down, sweating, and coming to, she caught a glimpse of Ernest's small arm pulling the door shut on his way out. The room was empty, except for her and Gracie. Staggering to the door, panting heavily, Ellie opened it and stepped into the hall.

"Ernest?" She questioned, for no logical reason. She hunched over and gasped for air as the eight kids turned the gray corner in solidarity, making their way, she was sure, to the Principal's office.

Jacqueline Vogtman

Father, Son, Ghost

Once they cross the Bridge of Flowers, Thomas knows there's no turning back. Beside him, Mark grips the steering wheel with meaty hands and stares at the road with an intensity Thomas has seen only when his brother was at bat at the end of a big game, when he was his high school's only hope. Thomas watches the picture-taking tourists and the drooping pink and yellow blooms that twine the parapet of the bridge recede in the side mirror, and he wonders what lies ahead.

This morning, as Thomas was walking back from Mass at Holy Family Seminary, where he's lived since he began school in the fall, he spotted Mark in the parking lot, sitting in his rusty Charger, its exhaust coughing faintly, like his father's muffled coughing Thomas used to hear sometimes in the bedroom next door—before, before. When Thomas approached the car Mark rolled down the window and didn't say *hi*, didn't greet his brother like he hadn't seen him in weeks, but immediately told him to get a bag. To put in it not clothes but any of the following: tape, rope, ski masks, hunting knife, paint, camera, socks, garbage bags, a photo of their mother. Thomas told him he had hardly any of those things, but Mark—looking older than his eighteen years, unshaven, eyes red-rimmed and squinting against the wind as if it were winter and not late spring—said to bring whatever he had. And hurry. They had a long trip ahead of them.

Thomas wasn't in the habit of questioning his brother, who's a year younger than him but has always seemed so much older; he did what he said, got in the car, and it was only after Mark pulled away from the seminary grounds and began driving the mountain roads, through towns of steeples and peaks to the eastbound highway, that he revealed to Thomas the skeleton of his plan. They were driving to a small seaside town near Cape Cod. To find their father, who left their family three weeks ago. But it wasn't their father Mark wanted to see; it was his lover, a man they've never seen, only heard. Heard yelling *cunt* and *fuck* and *bitch*, about their mother, in the background when they phoned their father that first night he left, when he told them he was gay, when they begged him to come back for the sake of their mom. He said no. He said he stuck around until they both turned eighteen and he did his duty.

It wasn't so long ago—a month, maybe?—that Thomas felt himself still a child. But riding beside his brother now, speeding down the highway, backseat strewn with baseball bats and cigarette cartons and beer bottles stolen from their dad's leftover stash, Thomas feels older, as if sadness and anger and the possibility of violence are what make one a man. He shifts in his seat, looks again in the side mirror at the road behind them. He can't shake the feeling he left something back there, at the seminary, some unanswered question, something bothering him during prayer. Mark accelerates, the speedometer creeping close to ninety. Thomas wants to ask him to slow down but doesn't, and as they race down the road every mile marker they pass looks like a white feather, as if the brothers are birds leaving a trail back to where they came from.

The seaside houses look like they're made of candy. Many are cottages, compact and covered with gumdrop-colored stones, while others are tall and perched precariously on thin columns resembling candy canes. As they drive down the roads into the town where their father resides with the man he's been having an affair with for the past year, the man he told his family he is in love with, Thomas feels a sense of vertigo, worries a strong wind might topple those tilting houses right onto their car. He tells this to his brother, joking, but Mark doesn't reply. He stares at the vacationers who walk and bicycle down the street, distractedly taps the steering wheel off-beat to the music on the tape player, some metal band whose name Thomas imagines is Slayer or Killer or Thrasher or Smasher. Thomas prefers Bach or the Beatles; he turns it down.

"What are you looking for?" he asks his brother. "Do you even know where this guy lives?"

Again, Mark doesn't answer, but reaches over and opens the glove compartment, taking out an envelope that has obviously been crumpled and then smoothed out and which bears the distinct mark of having been stomped on with muddy cleats. He points at the return address.

"He sent it to us a week ago," Mark says, then snorts. "With a fucking fifty dollar bill."

"So that's where they live?"

"A fucking fifty dollar bill," Mark continues. "Like that'll pay for our food and bills when Mom doesn't even work."

Thomas closes the glove compartment, cradles the envelope on his lap.

"What did he write in the letter?"

"I don't know—I didn't read it," Mark replies. "All I know is that Mom was crying afterward."

Thomas thinks of their mother, tiny woman who survived a

violent upbringing in Northern Ireland, who before their father left constantly reminded them how lucky they were to live in a peaceful country, how lucky she was to be taken care of so well by her husband who chose to marry her a year after she got to America, when she worked at a pub frequented by him and his college friends. Thomas imagines the way she looks when she cries: red splotches all over her face like she's been slapped hard by tiny hands, the clear rivulets of snot that drip from her nose, hang from the curved tip like icicles, like tusks. How ugly! And yet—this ugliness made him love her more, made him, for a moment, hate his father.

Mark snatches the envelope from his lap. "Sandpiper Road," he reads, looking over at the street signs. "Have you seen that yet?"

Thomas shakes his head. "Do you have any idea where it is?"

"Nah," Marks says. "But I'll find it." And he swings a sharp right into the tiny lot of a general store.

"What are you doing here?" Thomas asks, afraid of the impulsivity of his brother, who, growing up, more than once smashed holes in a wall of the bedroom they shared by hitting it with a baseball bat and then quickly covered up by painting over it with whatever color paint they had lying around the house: blue, yellow, violet, so that eventually their wall resembled a rainbow of bruised flesh. Their father had hated that, Mark's colorful walls. He was strict, straitlaced, until the day he left.

"I have to get a few things," Marks says, slamming the door, and then, through the open window: "I'm also gonna ask for directions to that place. You want anything? Grape soda, pretend it's wine, like the old days?"

Thomas smiles weakly, shakes his head, and his brother walks into the store, the bell above the door tinkling like the bells rung during Mass, as if the significance of this trip has made their every movement a sacrament. Thomas rolls his window down so he can stick his head out and smell the sea air. There's the faint odor of fish and then the scent of sunscreen wafting from the car parked next to them, where a girl rubs lotion over her freckled chest and shoulders. He averts his gaze, reaches under his shirt to caress the crucifix that lies there against his breastbone. It was a gift from his father before he entered the seminary, when he told Thomas that at one time he, too, had considered becoming a priest, a statement that now carries more hidden meaning, more complications. When his father first left and Thomas took the train home to comfort his mother, he thought about getting rid of the crucifix, burying it somewhere in the back yard near where he and Mark had buried and had makeshift funerals for countless pets when they were children: mice, rabbits, salamanders, frogs, even a snake. But he couldn't bring himself to do it.

He reads the smooth hills and hollows of the crucifix like brail: there's feet, torso, face, outstretched arms. And as sometimes happens, a prayer begins to form in Thomas' mind under other thoughts, the prayer itself buried like a dead animal that slowly comes to life and digs its way out of the soil to breathe the surface air. Thomas doesn't know if prayer really forms in the mind or somewhere else entirely, some mysterious dark space inside the bones made of pre-memory memories, his mother's whispered prayers while he was still in utero, the dawn weekday Masses she brought him to so her prayers would always sway inside his blood, would become a part of his genetic makeup.

In the name of the Father, the Son, and the Holy Spirit. He begins and ends each prayer the same way, usually making the sign of the cross but embarrassed to do so in such a visible place, in his brother's car, a pretty girl nearby. And as the Lord's Prayer murmurs under his heartbeat, he remembers what he left at the seminary, the fixation troubling him throughout theology class last week and during the groggy Mass this morning: the mystery of the Holy Trinity. The other seminary students he lived with didn't seem to care, went home after theology class the evening they learned about it and drank cheap church wine and passed around a nudie mag. But it bothered Thomas. Made him doubt. If the Son is *begotten* of the Father, and the Holy Spirit proceeds from the Father and the Son, how is it possible that they are truly One Being? Those words *begotten* and *proceeds* imply time and change, imply that the Trinity was not always one. A conundrum, a contradiction for the church. Never resolved, merely pushed aside. His teacher brought it up casually in class—one lesson devoted to readings on the Holy Trinity—but it was the one thing so far that has caused Thomas to question his faith and his place at the seminary to the point where he's considered returning home at the end of the semester, never to come back. Nothing else has made him question his choice to be a priest, not the high school crushes on quiet girls with names like Annabelle and Albertine, not scandals in the church, not even his father admitting he's gay. Those are surface problems. Fleeting. But the problem of the Trinity...

Mark returns to the car, dropping two plastic bags in the backseat before getting in the driver's side. He hands Thomas a piece of paper.

"I got directions," he says, and Thomas looks down at the scrawl of his brother's hand, the misspellings that litter the list of turns and street names. Mark smiles before he backs out, a wild smile, teeth sharp and crooked, lips too cracked to be spreading that wide.

"Here we go," he says.

Thomas glances back at the bags; through their transparency he can see rope, fishing line, duct tape, various knives, fishing hooks. Next to the bags are the bats, wooden and metal. He thinks of his brother's swing, the power behind it, how it bruised the walls of their home, how it could crush a man's skull. He looks over at Mark.

"What are we doing here, really?"

Mark drives slowly, staring at street signs. "We're just going to threaten him."

"You mean, Dad's...friend?" Thomas was going to say *lover* or *boyfriend*; too strange.

Mark nods.

"Not Dad?"

"No, not Dad," Mark says. "Though he's lucky I'm not coming for him too."

"I'm not sure this is the best idea," Thomas says. "I don't think I want to be part of this."

"You don't need to do any of the threatening. I'll take care of that."

"Then what do you even need me here for?"

"I just wanted your blessing," Mark says, then laughs. "I figure if you're here, nothing bad will happen."

"That's it?"

"Well, also, if something bad *does* happen, you'll have my back, right?"

Thomas nods, considers how best to dissuade him. They drive up and down streets close to shore, late afternoon sun glittering on the windows of houses as if they're covered with sugar. Thomas watches men coming back to these houses from the beach, their bodies pink, hairy, soft bellies above the waistline of their trunks vulnerable, swelling as if with the envy of pregnancy, sad reminders that they have held nothing inside of them save their own food and fat, they have never been one with someone else. Further on, young men and women are dressed up to walk the pier, and the lights of the restaurants and clubs blink on. Thomas spots an older man walking among the group of twenty-somethings, a man tall and balding like their father, wearing purple pleather pants and a tight shirt unbuttoned to the waist revealing gray chest hair, also like their father's.

It's him, possibly. No—probably. In three weeks he's become a stranger, a man who looks like he could be wearing nail polish. Thomas has the urge to laugh, to point him out to Mark, make a crack like, *Doesn't this guy know that gay people don't dress like that anymore?* But he can't speak. He feels a pang of pity in his gut, that soft place that will never hold anything other than his own organs and blood, that will never serve to unite him with another person.

The man that could be his father is so much older than the crowd around him and dressed like some disco-era drag queen, stooped over slightly, trying desperately to fit into this other world, this other world where he thinks he belongs and so obviously doesn't. Thomas continues to stare at him, and the almost neon colors of his dad's clothes make the others fade into the seascape, so that he sees his father walking along the pier alone, one solitary man close enough to call out to, to shout to him, *Here I am!* as he and Mark once did in childhood games of hide-and-seek, not wanting to wait so long to be found. But he'd never hear them, anyway, above the sound of the waves.

Mark has not seen their father, continues to stare at the street signs, and Thomas is glad, afraid of what Mark may have done had he seen him there, all glitter and glam and glaring separateness.

"Hey," Thomas says. "You're not going to hurt anyone, right?"

Mark laughs, says nothing.

"There're some words for that, you know," Thomas continues. "Gay bashing. Hate crime."

Mark stops laughing. "That's not what this is about."

"What, then?"

"Revenge. Justice. Honor." Mark pauses between each word, lighting a cigarette, taking a drag.

"Who do you think you are, Sir Galahad?"

Mark laughs again. "Dude, I don't even know who that is."

"What about your scholarship? Boston? You'll be throwing that away if you go to jail."

Mark doesn't reply.

"And your girlfriend?"

"Candice."

"Right, Candice. What about her?"

Mark flicks ash out the window. "None of that's important right now," he says. "Listen, if you want to get out of this, I'll drop you off somewhere and you can let me go on my own."

Thomas looks again at the pier. His father—or the man that resembled him—is gone. He glances at Mark's profile, his nose crooked from the times he's broken it throughout the years. Always the one getting in trouble, scraping the same knee over and over. Thomas always the one helping him up off the sidewalk.

"No," Thomas says. "I'll keep going with you. Just don't do anything stupid."

"I can't make any promises," Mark replies, and he flicks the cigarette out the window as he makes a turn, its fiery head getting lost for a moment in the blaze of golds and reds and pinks that covers everything in front of them.

• • •

It's nearing dusk when the brothers reach Sandpiper Road, a line of houses that leads to the beach, and when they roll up in front of the last house—their father's?—and Mark parks his car in a hidden spot behind a bush, they hear waves, their gentle roar like from the jaws of a distant lion. The house is small, with cupcake-shaped shutters, pastel piping along the roof, and one whitewashed side facing the sea. Such a cute house, while their mother can barely put food on the table. For a moment Thomas wonders why he's still here, why he hasn't talked Mark out of it yet. Maybe he wants to see his father's lover hurt. Maybe he wants to see his father hurt.

"Now what?" Thomas asks.

"We wait," Mark replies and turns to grab bags from the backseat. He takes out a ski mask, pulls it over his head. He looks at Thomas and asks, "Whaddya think?"

"I think it's strange that you feel the need to cover your face," Thomas says, "if you say you aren't planning on doing anything illegal." He studies his brother's eyes, piercing blue against surrounding black wool. Will their father recognize him by only his eyes or the shape of his face under the mask?

"I got one for you, too," Mark says, tossing a hat onto Thomas' lap. Thomas doesn't put it on, instead fishes his hands into a bag, pulling out a coiled yellow rope, holding it up in the fading light. He asks his brother what it's for.

Mark grabs it from him and puts it back in the bag. "We probably won't need it," he says. "I got it just in case."

"Just in case what?"

"In case someone needs to be restrained."

Thomas puts his head in his hands. Deep breath. The air through the window is so salty Thomas can feel it coating his skin, curling his hair, entering his mouth and nose, the landscape leaking into him.

"Does Mom know you're doing this?"

"Speaking of Mom," Mark replies, "do you have that picture I asked you to get?"

"You didn't answer my question," Thomas says, but digs into his book bag, pulling out a photograph. In it, their mother stands smiling behind Mark as he blows out candles for his third birthday. Behind them, a figure in the shadows, their father leans in the doorway.

Thomas hands the photo to Mark, who looks at it and says, "That's the only one you could find? One with *him* in it?"

"He's in them all," Thomas replies. "He might be in the background, but he's in them all. Besides, you can barely see him."

Mark sticks the photo in a corner of the dashboard, then nods his head and says, "Actually, this is good."

"What's the photo for, anyway?" Thomas asks.

"Inspiration," Mark answers, then opens his door. "Come on," he says.

Thomas gets out of the car and stretches his legs, looking out at the gray waves foaming on the sand. The salt air, the cramped legs at last free—it's reminiscent of childhood trips, and if Thomas could block out just one tiny corner of his mind, he could almost believe that is what they are doing right now, simply coming to the seashore for a family vacation as they do—as they did—every summer.

Mark opens the door to the back seat, gestures for Thomas to come over.

"Pick one." Mark points at the bats. Then he sighs shakily, looks over at their father's house. "Shit. I don't know what to do." He pats his sweatshirt pocket. Thomas notices a small bulge under the worn fabric, wonders if he's imagining it, and considers asking Mark what it is. But when he looks at his brother, he sees Mark's eyes are watering, almost crying, something Thomas hasn't seen him do in years and even when they were children was tough to watch, Thomas wanting to cry along with him as if tears were contagious, like yawns. Before Thomas can say anything, Mark looks away from the house, roughly rubs his eyes.

"Pick one," he repeats. "Just for protection. Just in case I need some help."

Thomas picks a wooden bat with a crack down the middle, and Mark looks at him quizzically, shakes his head and picks his own, the Louisville Slugger that Thomas knows won Mark's team the state championship.

"Now we just wait for them to come home," Mark says, leaning against the car, facing the beach. Thomas does the same.

"What if they're already home?"

"Then we'll just wait for them to come out if it takes all night," Mark says, squinting in the distance to see two teenage girls in cotton-candy pink bathing suits emerge from the waves, dripping wet and running up the dunes to return to their house.

"How could anyone not like women?" Mark says, turning to Thomas.

Thomas shrugs, looks away from the girls and at seagulls pecking a long line of detritus.

"I mean, you like girls, right?" Marks asks, glancing down at his hands, picking at the dirt under his nails. A wave crashes, and then a long hushing silence as the surf is sucked back in.

"What are you asking me?" Thomas replies. "If I'm gay?"

Mark chews on his thumbnail and Thomas walks to the passenger side, gets in, closes the door quietly, as he always does when he is angry, the angrier he is, the quieter. Mark comes in after him.

"I didn't mean anything by it," he says. "I just figured, you being a priest and all, and you never had a girlfriend…"

"First of all, I'm not a priest. Yet. Maybe I'll never be."

"So you *do* like women."

Thomas leans his head against the dashboard, groaning, "Holy shit, you're stupid."

Mark laughs and shoves him so that his shoulder hits the door. "You swore! You better say a prayer or something."

"Shut up," Thomas says and shoves his brother back. He can feel himself smiling, the first time he felt like smiling in the past three weeks, maybe the first time since he left home for the seminary.

And then, out of the corner of his eye, Thomas spots a car turning into the driveway of their father's house.

"Duck!" Mark hisses, and Thomas does, closing his eyes and then opening them, staring down at the Gatorade bottles and PowerBar wrappers that litter the floor of the car. He turns to Mark, whose head is leaning on the bottom of the steering wheel. He breathes heavily, hands twisting around the neck of the baseball bat that lies across his lap.

"I'm getting out," he whispers. "You should too, but hide behind the car. I'm gonna have a few words with the guy."

"Shouldn't I come with you?"

"No," Mark answers. "You just keep watch and make sure things don't get too heavy. If they do, step in."

Thomas feels his hands grow sweaty around the bat.

"We can still leave, you know," Thomas says, but he sees his brother tense up as if he's ready to spring, pull the ski mask down over his face, and then he pops open the door and runs out silent and stealthy, holding the bat as if to bunt. Thomas opens his own door and rolls out, kneels in the sandy road, peering over the hood of the car. His father has already walked up to the porch—it was not him, after all, in the purple leather pants an hour ago. He's dressed as he always used to dress in the summer: shorts, sandals, Hawaiian shirt. Lagging behind him, another man—his lover? his partner? his boyfriend? no name seems right—exits the car and begins to walk up the driveway. Thomas can't see his face, but from the back the man is short, stocky, with pale veiny calves and white hair. This is him? The man who broke up their family? This man who looks like he might be somebody's grandfather, who looks like those men who come to church every Sunday wearing mothballed suits and hats with feathers stuck in the brim, who drop nickels in the collection basket?

Thomas sees Mark hesitate at the bottom of the driveway, and it's a moment, Thomas knows, that could change everything. But then Mark calls to the old man, "Hey, you!" The man turns around, takes a step toward Mark and then begins backing away. Maybe it's something mean—or sweet—in his face that compels Mark to lift the bat from his side and, like a sneeze, a blink, a jerk of the knee, swing and crack the man right in the ribs. The man falls to the driveway curled like a fetus, and Thomas can hear Mark bellowing between hits, something about their mother, their family, but his voice is slight, half its power stolen by the sea.

Thomas wants to call to Mark and tell him to come back, to leave now before anything else happens, but he's paralyzed when he sees something black and shiny fall out of Mark's sweatshirt pocket as he swings, and he remembers Mark patting that pocket earlier as he was tearing up. *Just for protection*, Mark had said about the bats, but he could have just as well been talking about a gun. Thomas stands, ready to run and pick up the gun and drag his brother back to the car, but his father runs up instead, grabs the gun off the gravel. The three men in front of Thomas look like strangers, figures in a painting, and he glances from each to each, wondering which one needs his protection most.

Thomas rushes forward and calls out to Mark, but his voice is overcome by two loud cracks, which he's not sure is the sound of a bat against a man's skull or the sound of a gun going off. But then he sees Mark drop to the ground next to the writhing old man, his brother's body twitching, and the source of the noise dimly registers in Thomas' mind.

Their father rushes forward, kneels down beside Mark and peels off his ski mask, bowing over his son's body with the pain of recognition. He's crying out, but his voice, too, seems unreal as the wind distances it and the crash of waves snuffs it out. Blood washes over sand, stones, elements that don't know blood from seawater. Whose blood? His brother's, his father's, this other man's? His own? No way to know just by looking.

Thomas feels he's floating as he walks forward, as if into a frieze on the wall of a church. His father holds his limp brother in his arms. Mark's baseball bat rolls into the street, cracked in half by soundless, invisible lightning. Thomas doesn't know whether he should drive away, or call the cops, or carry his brother back to the car, or finish his brother's job. Which path to take? Not one seems right; not one fixes what's wrong.

In the failing light, Thomas can barely see his father's face looking up at him. Thomas is close enough to touch them, his father and brother, but he won't. Everything seems unknowable, untouchable, and his fists are unable to grasp the gun his father tries to hand him. The gun drops to the sand silently and glimmers in the moonlight a moment.

And there, in the middle of the street, beneath the clockwork of thoughts, somewhere in the eternal silence of his blood or bones, Thomas remembers the story his mother told him on the phone the other night when he confessed to her that he was questioning his faith, the parable of Saint Augustine on the shore trying to find the answer to the question of the Trinity. Walking along the beach, she said, Augustine met a child who was running back and forth from the waves, using a seashell to try to scoop the entire sea into a tiny opening in the sand. Augustine laughed and told him it was impossible to displace the whole ocean. Not nearly as impossible, the child answered, as you trying to understand the mystery of the Holy Trinity.

And then the child disappeared.

Lee Matthew Goldberg

Our Buick Stopped Here

Colt's fingers crept towards the silver combination lock of his daddy's suitcase. From the front seat of their car, his daddy reached back and swatted Colt's hand away with a grimace of twisted yellow teeth. *No funny stuff* said his daddy's eyes in the rear view mirror, but *funny stuff* was what Colt did best. They had stopped in front of a house on a quaint, tree-lined block that Colt found familiar to his own—a slow moving world of nosy neighbors, tossed newspapers, and jingling ice cream trucks. His daddy then changed his tune and teased him by sliding a quarter from behind his ear. Colt knew better. Loose change wouldn't buy good behavior. He let the sweaty quarter plop into his palm, but kept his other hand in a hidden caress of the suitcase and waited patiently for his daddy to disappear.

"Watch your sister," his daddy said, rubbing his stubbly cheeks.

Colt's sister Louise was occupied in the front seat with her dolly. She softly sang a made-up song about how much she was in love with it. She combed its long blond hair and pretended it was a mermaid by creating an ocean out of the air. Colt thought she was dumb.

His daddy twiddled his fingers in a wave to her, but she was transfixed with the flaxen hair of the dolly and answered him only in a sigh. His daddy then stepped out of the car and turned his hat around in his hands like a steering wheel.

"You both behave now," he called out.

Colt studied the way every feature on his daddy's face was pressed towards the middle, making his swelled head look like a balloon. He wondered if his own facial features would move towards the center as he got older. He promised then to stretch his eyes and mouth away from his nose before bed each night.

His daddy reached the front steps and rang a doorbell. Colt heard it play a pretty tune while his daddy jammed his hands into his pockets, rocked back and forth, and whistled with the tune. The door opened and the embrace of a woman's silk scarf flung around his neck. He shimmied inside. Once his daddy was out of sight, Colt heard the suitcase's lock singing to him. He counted eight slow Mississippis, which was his age; then it would be safe to listen to the call of the lock again.

The sun smoothed over the top of their brown Buick as Colt's curious fingers moved closer to the lock. He knew the combination from paying careful attention each time it was opened. The morning broke over the Nebraska countryside causing his right side to tingle from the warmth. His goose pimples disappeared, and he twitched until he felt more relaxed. The dusty front and back windows of the car let in a light littered with thousands of particles that looked like tiny gnats. He stuck his hand over his eyes, but all he could do was to squint and deal with its rays.

They had been in the car for two days straight, and the smell of gas and old leather was making him nauseous. He had shared the backseat with Louise last night, but she had a bad dream and kicked him in the face. He yanked a few blond hairs out of her head and she cried. Their daddy woke up, took her side as always, and Colt slept in a patch of dirt by the car's exhaust pipe.

After making sure that Louise wasn't watching him, he spun the lock around to the right numbers. He blinked nervously and imagined his daddy could hear everything he was doing from inside the house, believing that because his daddy was older, he naturally had powers that surpassed his own. His daddy could hear, smell and see with a superhuman ability that made Colt feel like he was being monitored at all times.

The lock finally let out a slow, loud *ssssnnnaaapppp*, reminding him of when his friend Samuel dared him to break a chicken's neck. Samuel's family had a farm on the other side of town. Samuel held the clucking, crying chicken between his knees that day. Colt squeezed his eyes shut as the chicken flapped like a madman, then he wrapped his hands around the chicken's warm neck and twisted until it became limp and cold. The memory made his goose pimples return.

The suitcase had a musty smell that was stronger once opened. It smelled a lot like Colt's daddy, who would sweat rings around his armpits, even in the middle of winter. He saw that a bottle of Old Spice cologne had spilled over a bunch of shiny black connected packets. They looked like lollypop wrappers with writing over them, but didn't have sticks like lollypops do. He felt one between his fingers and slipped it in his pocket.

"Daddy's not gonna like it, daddy's not gonna like it," Louise sang. She slowly combed her dolly's hair and scowled at him in the side mirror. Colt paid her no mind.

The rest of the suitcase was filled with old sweaters, a pair of khakis, a Bible, a shaving kit, a dirty magazine, and the utensil gadget that his daddy invented and sold door-to-door. His daddy had spent hours on it in the basement when they had one and talked about how it was going to *revolutionize American eating*. It was a vibrating knife and fork in one. The knife part came out from one end and the fork part came out from the other. It always bothered his daddy that people had to use both hands to eat: one to spear the food, and the other to cut it with. Colt never saw that as a problem. It also didn't look like a utensil, but more like this mess of an art project that this girl at his old school had made out of a potato. Colt had made an ashtray for his mom.

He hoped to find a picture of his mom in the suitcase. He knew his dad kept one. He missed her. Even though there were bad times as well as good ones, at least some used to be good. They only became bad recently when she would cry all the time, pull out her hair, and even forget his name. He was told that she went on a vacation and they wouldn't see her for a long while. Colt loved vacations more than anything. His family went once a year to Pawnee Lake in Lincoln, but had skipped it that summer. His mother would pack the greatest picnic baskets ever with cream cheese and jelly sandwiches on raisin bread. It made him so hungry to think about the sandwiches. His daddy told them earlier they had to skip breakfast to make good time.

Colt wanted the picture of his mom in high school. She had long brown hair with a part down the middle and was blowing a kiss to the camera. She told Colt that her old boyfriend took the picture after the two of them decided in their pre-calculus class to get married. The picture was taken after the bell rang and they were on their way. Colt couldn't believe that someone other than his daddy had ever been with his mom. He imagined them growing up together.

He would've continued to search though the suitcase, but he heard the front door to the house slam. His daddy waddled out like a clumsy penguin. He was pretty short for a grownup, and Colt almost came up to his shoulder. It made Colt laugh to think about his uncles calling his daddy *stool*. They'd lean on his daddy with loud laughs until he'd curse, stomp his feet, and push them away. Then they'd say, "C'mon, stool, don't be such a stick in the mud." He'd yell back, "*Shaddup* with all of you," and mutter to himself like Oscar the Grouch did when the real people knocked on his garbage can.

Colt could see his daddy muttering to himself, which meant that he was either really happy, or something went wrong, so he quickly closed the forbidden suitcase. He locked it without taking his eyes off of his approaching daddy.

"Get out of the car," his daddy ordered, and swung their wide car door open. "We're going inside."

He said it first to Colt, and then nodded to Louise as well. She continued combing her dolly's hair without looking up until he gave her a good yank. She fit a hesitant fist into his hand. As they climbed the stairs to the house, they seemed so far away to Colt, like he was watching them through the wrong side of a pair of binoculars. He tagged along, foggy from the sun and travel with a queasy feeling like he didn't belong anywhere.

Once inside, the house smelled of kitty litter. Colt had had a cat named Scratches who was lost in the fire, which happened earlier that summer. Scratches' kitty litter box was kept in their bathroom and the piss and poop smell often sat in the hallway and found its way into Colt's bedroom. His daddy told him and Louise that Scratches was up in the sky with a million other cats and if they looked closely they could see him in a cloud. Colt was never able to see him. Even though Louise said she did, he didn't believe her. She just said it to show off to their daddy. Colt knew that Scratches was now just a pile of ash.

The heat made the house's smell even worse. Tiny electric fans throughout the living room whirred even hotter air against his face. The furniture was wrapped in plastic coverings, and Colt thought there were enough pictures of Jesus hanging on the walls to start a church. A bronze crucified Jesus hung by the staircase and was surrounded by about a dozen God's Eyes. The Jesus was sweating just as much as he was.

There was dirt in the stubs of his fingernails and dirt in a line where his T-shirt met his neck. There was dust engrained in his nostrils from driving through the back Nebraska roads. He hadn't taken a bath or a shower in days but that was fine with him. He wanted to take off his shirt and swim in Pawnee Lake where his family used to go on vacations. The water there was different than bathwater. It was warm and muddy, and left a heavy coated smell that weighed him down. He'd plug his nose and dip deep down until he sat underwater, imagining he was the ruler of the lake. It'd been a while since he'd done that. He was beginning to forget what it felt like.

He saw a woman appear from the kitchen and instantly wondered if her large size would cause her to sink in Pawnee Lake. She wore what looked like a big floral tablecloth with a hole in the middle for her head to fit through. Her hair was cut short and sat on her head like a bike helmet. She fanned herself with a placemat and unstuck the tablecloth from her wet and red neck. He noticed how her chubby feet were stuffed into her slippers, and it made him think of the way his mother used to tie up a roast before she placed it in the oven.

"Heeellllooo," the woman called in a sloppy wave. She charged at them and immediately engulfed Colt in her massive breasts. He felt them slap against his skull as he gulped for a breath. She ran her fingers along his scalp and felt the short blond hairs that stuck straight up. "My heavens, you are just so darling. What a handsome, handsome boy. You could be in the movies," she squealed, and headed over to Louise who welcomed the strangling hug like she needed it. Louise even chucked her dolly to the ground in exchange for being picked up.

"Oh, Hal," the woman said, and almost dropped Louise from being overly excited. "You showed me pictures, but your children are GORGEOUS. They should be in a catalog for some fancy clothes. My Sears catalog does not have children that look like this."

She grabbed Colt's chin and shook it back and forth. He felt her fingernails scrape against the corner of his mouth and didn't like it. His mother's nails were never sharp because she bit them. They felt smooth against his cheeks when she pulled him close.

"Do you like dolls?" the woman asked, and Colt raised his head up but realized she was talking to Louise.

"This is my mermaid," Louise said, and picked up her dolly. The woman clasped her hands together and settled them on her stomach with a chuckle.

"C'mon, pumpkin, I have a whole collection of Marie Osmond dolls from QVC. They're exquisite. I just love her." She swiped Louise's hand and they disappeared up the stairs.

His daddy curled his hand around the edge of the banister and swung his body to get a full view of the woman walking up the stairs. He stared at her big butt, which Colt thought looked like two honeydews. He noticed how hard she stepped and how her thick legs made it sound like she was jumping up and down on the floor above him.

"She's what's called a desperate woman," his daddy whispered. "The best thing about one of them is they'll grab onto anything over being alone. Even me. Even you."

"What would she grab us for?" Colt asked but was ignored.

"Like this house?" his daddy asked, and licked his lips with a wink. He glided his hand down the banister until it touched Colt on the shoulder. Colt nodded. "Lot like our old house, no? We had one of those."

He pointed over to a lopsided record player. Colt thought of his mother dancing from the kitchen to a song about a Sweet Caroline. His daddy used to call her that.

"You used to sing to mom," Colt said, but his daddy either didn't hear him or feel like responding again.

"What would you say to a nice, big meal? A home cooked one, bud? What would you say to that?"

120

His daddy rubbed his little potbelly and licked his lips some more. Colt imagined a huge turkey that sizzled as it left the oven with chestnut apple stuffing and yams with marshmallows. He imagined it in his old house, though, not this one. His daddy led him into the kitchen as the kitty litter smell disintegrated. It was replaced by the warm familiar scent a kitchen has of a thousand meals cooked.

The kitchen was small and reminded him of a family's on television. It was bright, sparkling, and filled with cheap knick-knacks of the Lord. The woman also had ceramic birds hanging from the walls and in the outlines of her wallpaper. Four chairs were set around a table with three place mats, four glasses, and his daddy's utensil gadget at each setting. A meaty smell leaked from the oven. Colt's stomach growled like an alley cat in heat.

Something brushed up against the back of his neck. He never expected his daddy to pull him close with a hug. He got a whiff of Old Spice and smiled because Louise wasn't getting a hug at that moment. His daddy was only thinking of him.

A few minutes later, the woman came down still fanning herself with a place-mat and then finally left it on the table. Louise scurried along behind and clung onto the woman's dress with a tight fist. A new doll rested in her other arm.

The woman opened the oven as their meal overpowered everything else in the room. Colt closed his eyes and tasted juicy turkey with a cup of fatty gravy, thick like syrup, to wash it all down. His mom always told him to *eat whatever you want to, 'cause when you're dead, it won't matter if you were fat or skinny. Ya might as well have lived while you had the chance.* He caught a glimpse of the woman's stomach that looked like the inner tube he once brought on vacation. He guessed she lived by that saying as well and ate whatever the heck she wanted to.

There was no turkey though. The woman placed a big shaking piece of Spam casserole in front of him. It jiggled around like Jell-O, and the wonderful smell from the oven was defeated by the thought of cutting out chunks from a pig's stomach. His nostrils filled with zoo smells, and across the table Louise's face gave off the impression that her new dolly's head had been ripped off.

"How come things smell good until you see them in front of you?" Colt asked, to no one in particular.

His daddy tucked a napkin into his shirt and picked his ear with his pinky. His pinky shook so fast it reminded Colt of the time his cousin's dog had a seizure.

"Colt, we are polite at dinner table. Now say some grace."

Colt saw his daddy put the same pinky in his mouth and wondered if the large woman thought that was disgusting like he did. She bowed her head down an inch above her shaking Spam casserole and waited patiently for the Lord's Prayer. Colt cleared his throat.

"God bless the bounty of food we have today and hope that tomorrow we should be as blessed as we are now. God bless daddy, and…ma…and Louise I guess, my baseball glove, and nice lady for letting us into her home. Amen."

He felt the woman take his hand. Her hand was so big compared to his own that his fit completely inside. When she finally let go, he thought his own would forever be sweaty. She looked at him like she wanted to eat him up right at that very moment.

"That was beautiful, Colt, just touching. God gave you a gift with words, He really did. You might consider becoming a preacher."

Colt's eyes lit up from that remark. He liked being told that he was good at things.

"And my name is Nora. You can always call me Nora."

"My mom is in an intuition," Colt sang out, as the woman crinkled her nose.

"Institution, dear. It's called an institution."

The dinner wasn't as bad as Colt expected. The meat was airy, rubbery, and tasted like someone made a meatloaf out of old bologna. He was starving, though, and would have been pleased as punch with anything. His daddy made them all try the utensil gadget, but it was really difficult to use and Colt's mushy meat kept collapsing from the gadget's intense shake. Nora laughed every time she turned it on and it vibrated. She whispered closely in his daddy's ear a lot. He gave her a nod and wink while massaging her neck.

Soon the meat had settled in his stomach and felt like a submarine torpedo that was waiting to blow. He felt embarrassed about farting in front of Nora because he didn't know her and she might think it was rude. But then his daddy made a big fart and Louise giggled. Nora rolled her eyes but she was giggling as well. Then he knew it was okay and gave a small fart too.

"Do you like school?" Nora asked him after the farts died down. Louise answered her even though she wasn't the one asked.

"I'm gonna go to kindergarten and have my own pencils and pens at my new school," she said to her new doll.

"That's sweet," was all Nora said to that. Then she asked Colt again.

"I guess. My friends are at my old school, and I miss playing baseball with them. Don't know if I'll have any new friends. Don't know where my new school's gonna be. But I'm starting third grade when the summer ends and I like raising my hand and answering the teacher's question right."

"Do you get the right answer often?"

"Yes."

"Sometimes we have to move on," his daddy said, but Nora swatted his hand as if it was a fly.

"Couldn't I take a school bus to my old school?" Colt asked.

"Colt, no bus is about to drive four hundred miles to ship you to and from school each day. Schools are all the same. You'll go to school right around here, and you'll make new friends 'cause kids are all the same. Enough of this talk. Too much talk ain't good."

His daddy's words were slurred because he was trying to pick a piece of Spam out of his two front teeth. He had a big gap between them and a piece wedged in good. Colt wondered what he meant about too much talk. It made him inch down in his seat and think hard about not saying anything until he was directly spoken to.

But then he had a super idea. He could feel the lollipop-like thing from the suitcase in his back pocket. He would show his daddy how cool his new invention was. He excused himself politely from the table and took his glass of fruit punch with him. Nora and his daddy were playing with each other's fingers, and Louise was making faces at her Spam casserole. No one had noticed he'd left.

In her living room, he opened the lollypop-like wrapper and pulled out a white circle of rubber. He studied it for a moment and realized it was definitely a traveling cup for someone on-the-go. All one had to do was pinch the tip of the rubber thing and pull it through to make it longer. He poured in some fruit punch and it expanded like a balloon but held solid. His daddy was a regular genius. He would be so happy to see how his invention had worked. Colt thought he was so smart to make instant cups that you could fit into your pocket and use whenever you were thirsty.

Colt galloped back into the kitchen and carefully held the juice in his newfound cup. His daddy was going to give him an even bigger hug than when they first entered the kitchen. The door swung him inside as he held up his daddy's invention for everyone to see.

"Look, daddy! Look at your invention! Look what it can do!"

Colt smiled so hard he felt the ends of his mouth strain from being stretched, but he didn't care. Nora was laughing so much that tears leaked from her eyes. His daddy wasn't smiling though. He came toward him, and Colt raised the hand that wasn't holding the rubber cup out to hug him. But his daddy's palm flew into the air like it was asking a question and snapped forward at Colt with a sharp sting. The rubber thing spilled to the ground, and Colt stumbled to the floor shaking.

His short breath fired from his mouth like bullets. He was a soldier and had fallen. The enemy had surrounded him. He had taken a shot to his eye and it throbbed like when he stepped on a hornet's nest at summer camp and they fed on him. He closed his eyes to travel in his mind to Pawnee Lake. Once he saw it, he dove in. The muddy water was cold, consuming, and wonderful. On land he could hear Nora telling his daddy to calm down, but as he dove down further into the murky lake, he left the world on the surface and managed to smile. They must have all thought he went crazy.

Colt had a big knot like a tattoo over his eye. He winced in front of the bathroom mirror and dabbed rubbing alcohol on it. His nose was running and he sniffed hard, but he promised himself not to cry. Instead, he began stretching out his face. He took his cheeks between his fingers and pulled at them until it felt like his lips were about to tear. He then brushed his teeth with his index finger and smiled at himself. Louise was already tucked into bed when he entered their room.

"Daddy never said goodnight," she said. "Nora did."

Colt hovered over a lamp in the shape of a bird and turned on the light to annoy her.

"Big deal," he said.

Her eyes squinted at the bird's light.

"But now the bed bugs will bite."

"So let 'em. Just let 'em. You brush your teeth?"

She shook her head.

"Go brush, Louise, or your gums will fall out."

"It's dark and I'm scared." She inched down into the blankets until they were at level with her nose.

"I'll leave the lamp on for you."

She slid down fully into the blankets. Colt saw that a few wisps of blond fuzzy hair stuck out as the blankets shivered. He was in no mood for her.

"You better get used to it. We ain't leaving here for awhile."

They were silent, but Colt knew it was true. They had stayed with his daddy's friend Earl for a few weeks after the fire. They lived with baked beans and Vienna sausages for dinner. They lived in a mobile home and slept on sheets stained with beer. They lived with Earl's temper, and Colt got used to the back of his hand. None of his uncles wanted to have anything to do with his daddy anymore. His daddy spoke during those weeks of a woman he met on the road. He spoke of her as if she'd be their salvation. Colt knew that he better get used to her.

"There's a monster in the hallway," Louise said, sounding like a dying robot.

"The monster's in your mind." He sat down on the bed next to her and looked at the tiny lump she was. He lowered the blankets. Her face was wet and snot lingered around her nose. He grabbed a tissue from the nightstand and made her give a good blow.

"When are we going home?" she asked, and rubbed her sleeve across her face.

Colt turned to the quiet night outside. The crickets were talking to one another. He heard faint moans from the bedroom that his father and Nora had locked themselves into. The bruise over his eye felt prickly and tight. Louise reached out her tiny fingers to touch it. She was the only one who bothered to see if it hurt.

"We're not," he replied.

She looked at him confused.

"Fires don't bring houses back, Louise. They take them away. She's not coming back."

The moans from the other bedroom became louder until Colt plugged his ears with his sleeves. Louise's chin quivered and the tears were about to return. He didn't care.

"Go brush your darn teeth, Louise."

She crossed her arms in a huff of tears.

"Go!" he yelled, and gave her a small kick. He ripped the blankets off and picked her up out of bed. She bit his arm and left tiny teeth marks. She squealed and he clamped his hand over her mouth. He carried her into the bathroom as she fought and screamed. Maybe he wanted his father to hear. Maybe he wanted Nora to speak up. Maybe he wanted things to be different in this new family. He knew for certain that he'd be damned if Louise's gums fell out and made sure that each tooth got its fair share of scrubbing.

Colt dreamt endlessly that night; in clips, scenes, and fragmented collages, which melted into one another. He tossed wildly, became tangled up in his blankets and threw them across the room. His mind was in motion. The road always moved him somewhere else.

A bone-colored dusk with smoke in coiled patterns hung in the distance. He felt heat on his right side but the rest of him was chilled. Louise lay beside him in the backseat, asleep and forever innocent as he watched the last cinders of his childhood burn away. Mrs. Nelson and their son Eric were in the front. He and Louise were getting driven home from school that day after stopping for ice cream. Mrs. Nelson cried out like she was being tortured as the car rolled past Colt's crumbling house. Firemen and neighbors were stuck in the slow motion world that Colt created for the situation. He pressed his perspiring hands against the window as if to touch and hold onto the place he called home for an extra second. His mother was there with messy hair that hid her face. She was being led handcuffed into a police car that blipped through the approaching night and dragged her away. The words *crazy* and *ashamed* came from the neighbors watching the scene. Mrs. Nelson kept on driving and yelled at him not to watch, but he was caught forever in the moment's reality—the scattered pieces, the confusion and emptiness of it all, the feeling of knowing nothing could ever return to the way it was. And then the dream would begin again.

Dawn was breaking and morning felt cold and unfamiliar. Louise was still asleep and birds were chirping outside. Colt rubbed his eyes and didn't want to hear the birds. Waking up always left him dazed. He never liked his dreams to end. They were becoming less real as time went on. They were becoming the dreams of another.

No one was awake to appreciate the sunrise. The smell of coffee used to end his dreams as it escalated from his mother's breath when she woke him. Sometimes she led him outside to catch the sun. He'd still be carrying last night's sleep in his eyes as he grabbed for her hand. They'd settle at the foot of a hill: sleepy, frozen, but eager, and all of a sudden he would feel warm.

He went outside of Nora's house and sat in a patch of dirt. The sun was sharp and hot against his collar. He picked up a stick and started to draw with it. He heard the screen door slam behind him and turned around.

His father was at the door with a coat and a hat in his hands. He rotated the hat around in his stubby fingers and chewed on his lip. The hat fell to floor and his father bent to pick it up without taking his eyes off of him.

"Hey, Colt. Hey, spud. What you doing up?"

He waddled over to Colt and tapped him on the head like a puppy. Colt squinted at him with his red eye and continued to draw in the dirt. He was making a never-ending circle and stabbing deeper and deeper into the ground.

"Nuthin'."

"Well, spud, I was just…uh…going for some ice cream. Wanna join?"

Colt shook his head, but his father pulled him to his feet and took the stick away.

"There's this ice cream place on Main Street, Colt. Let me tell you that you have not tasted ice cream until you've tasted this ice cream. You can tell all your little friends that your daddy let you have ice cream for breakfast. How many kids get ice cream for breakf…"

"I don't have any friends."

"Nonsense."

His father led him to the Buick. Colt sat up front. The coat and the hat were thrown into the backseat on top of the suitcase. wished he was in the backseat and the coat and hat were next to his father. His father started the car and they bumped along the road.

"Why were you up so early?" Colt asked in a mope. His father let out a big exhale.

"What do you mean?"

"Where were you going?"

His father turned around to place a hand on his shoulder and try and shake the mope out of him before looking back at the road.

"Well, bud, sometimes grownups go through certain things. I know it's difficult to understand and that it's been a peculiar summer for you. Don't think that I haven't seen how you've changed. You're becoming a man."

Colt at that moment wanted his blanket from when he was a baby.

"What am I trying to say, Colt? Remember when we used to go on vacation? Remember those? Remember Pawnee…"

"With mom?"

"Yeah with…mom, with all of us. You would swim."

His father's lips spun wildly in different directions. He was trying hard to think of what to say next. Colt knew that was what he always did; he was forever stalling.

"I liked the lake," Colt mumbled to his hands.

"Well, your father needs a vacation. Your father needs a lake to go to and relax for a while. Don't even remember the last time I was able to sit back."

They pulled up in front of the ice cream parlor. His father snapped off the motor and led Colt inside by his neck. The inside was cool and made his goose pimples appear. The parlor had a buzz to it that the man behind the counter hummed along to.

"What do you do want, spud? Anything you want."

Colt wanted to leave. He wished he never woke up. The man was staring at his eye that buzzed along with the parlor. He felt like a mutant.

"Don't care."

"Sure you do. You like vanilla. Two vanillas," he said, to the humming man.

"I don't like that."

"You always liked vanilla. Got it the last time we got ice cream."

His father passed a vanilla cup to him. He devoured his own in a few gulps. The humming man whistled good-bye to them but Colt only frowned. It was hot when they stepped outside. The ice cream began to melt instantly. They stepped into the Buick and drove away.

"You're not eating yours?" his father asked.

Colt looked down at his puddle of vanilla.

"Not hungry."

"Don't have to be hungry to eat ice cream. All kids eat ice cream."

"Mom never let me have ice cream for breakfast. What'd she say if she knew?"

"Can't imagine she'd say much right now. Your mother's not for this world, Colt. Some people are better left in their own head."

Colt didn't respond. He listened to the crunching stones under the car. His father grabbed his vanilla cup at one point, slurped it up, and then threw the cup out of the window. They stopped in front of Nora's house, but his father kept the motor running.

"You know what you get to be?" his father asked, and smoothed down his wild strands of hair in the vibrating rear-view mirror.

"No."

"Man of the house. How many kids can say that?"

"Don't know."

"Well, not many. Not many at all. How's that sound?"

His father didn't even look at him. He was preoccupied with his cowlick that refused to go down. He kept spitting into his palm and stamping it over the cowlick with a grin.

"Well, someones gotta be it if you sure ain't," Colt said.

His father finally looked over and his smile faded into a frown.

Colt took that frown with him proudly and jammed his arm to open up the car door. He jumped outside, slammed the door, and refused to look back. The car sputtered for a moment, almost deciding what to do next before angrily rumbling away. Colt only turned around when it was just a little bug in the distance that he could swat away. He fit the car in the palm of his hand and gave it a good crunch.

They stayed with Nora for a while before bouncing around foster homes. She had waited for their father by the window for weeks, calling his name quietly. Eventually she just glanced at the window if she passed by, and soon she stopped looking at all. She couldn't afford two children on her own, and it was time for him and Louise to leave.

The next and last time Colt saw his father was at a car dealership in Omaha. Colt was nineteen and purchasing his first car. He was working as a mechanic and knew what he was looking for and what he could afford with a pregnant girlfriend and money needed towards fixing up her parent's basement as a starter home. He'd been taking care of Louise, too, a sophomore now in high school and a star swimmer, more at home in the water than anywhere else. She had long blond hair, a face still full of baby fat, and was difficult and prone to sneak out with local boys in the wheat fields, but they clung to each other despite any arguments, having shared a bond for years when they were all each other had.

When he entered the car dealership, a row of twisted yellow teeth welcomed him in as if he was royalty. His father never recognized who he was, which stung at first, but then Colt decided to screw with him. The years hadn't been kind to his father. He was a sweaty mess, mopping his brow continuously with a handkerchief. His potbelly hung far over his waistline, his breath stunk of liquor, and his eyes were bloodshot and desperate for a sale. He teased his father with offers way out of his price range all day, and in the end, left with nothing. He could tell his father was pissed, but he wouldn't have had it any other way.

Now and then throughout the years, he'd let his thoughts fly and glide back to calm and muddy Pawnee Lake, his reflection fading more and more against its sparkling surface. The sun would dangle above him like it was attached by string. He'd sink his toes into the grainy sand and the water would crawl up his feet and ankles. He'd slide into the lake and wade further and further out until his legs kicked through clumps of wet dirt, tickling his body and removing the sun's warmth. The water would be smelly like a sewer, but when he'd break through the surface, his mother would be waiting for him on land like a tiny bug in the distance. He never saw her again after the day of the fire. When he was a teenager, he finally found out what institution she was sent to, but she had already hung herself with her bed sheets, discovered by an orderly one morning swinging from the piping in the corner of her room.

But on the shore of his lake, she'd see him and wave with a cup of coffee in her other hand. As the years passed on, she became more and more hidden behind a screen of haze and smoke, her image full of scents, or the sound of her voice, but he began to lose her face. So he'd close his adult palm around her tiny self and try and hold on for as long as possible, squeezing his curious fingers with all his might until he remembered her pretty hazel eyes, her warm smile, or those coffee-scented kisses.

Each time he'd have to squeeze harder and harder to keep her there, but one day, just like that, there was nothing left to squeeze. So he started replacing those memories with the here and now, of his little girl Caroline wrapping her arms around his leg, and then his torso, and finally growing tall enough to be shoulder-to-shoulder.

Even once he became stooped over and needed to rest against her for support, he'd always try to look into her wide eyes and force himself to see the future instead of the past.

NONFICTION

Cindy Warren

Leroy

I didn't start out thinking much of him. A surly, black bus-driver in 1975 Las Vegas was just one more thing I had to endure. His roughhewn face appeared stony, and he was darker than the color of good chocolate. He looked mad about having to drive the east side students to the west side's Jo Mackey Sixth-Grade Center. We were part of the new city-wide integration program and the animosity it stirred up. Our city needed peacemakers.

They drew my name in the group who would be bussed across town, and Leroy drew the line with us on the first day of school. "This is my bus and it's a long drive. I expect you to sit quietly and stay seated. Understand?" His angry voice shook the bus.

Most of my friends had remained on the east side, so I whispered to the stranger sitting next to me, "We didn't even do anything, and he's already mad at us."

The desegregation program separated friends and stirred up hostility. Nobody that lived on the east side wanted their kids bussed over to the west side. The program also seemed futile. I'd experienced the east side schools and knew that bussing the west side students over wouldn't improve their education. Most of my teachers were unmemorable or worse.

I had the senile and stupid Mrs. Anderson in second grade. She asked us constant questions about etiquette. Then there was Mr. Frye, a ferocious bore who taught fifth. He paraded up and down the aisles, whacking our fingers and jamming his ruler into our backs. As expected, our sixth grade teachers were no worse than those I'd had on the east side. One of the things I most remember about that year was the music. K.C. and the Sunshine Band was huge in '75. "That's the Way I Like It" and "Get Down Tonight" blared every time I turned on the radio. The music helped bring the east side and west side students together. While waiting in line to play tetherball, we'd all sing words we were too young to understand. Tall, gangly, and undeveloped, I felt out of place like a giraffe at a petting zoo. That was not the way I liked it.

The up side to the integration program was the cultural diversity. The black students always had the best new words. When Dad relayed stories about his mean boss, I'd say, "That's cold-blooded." For a short time, I even had three short, black admirers. This little group of boys used to try to "cop a feel." I suffered their antics in good humor because they were cute, and because I knew they'd quickly move on. I had nothing to grope.

On the bus ride home three black girls, who also lived on the east side, were sitting behind me. Apparently, they didn't like the attention I'd been receiving. They started thumping me on the back of the head.

"Stop it!" I demanded.

Gleeful laughs accompanied each new thump. As I slunk deeper in my seat, I felt powerless to stop them and afraid to tell Leroy. The intensity escalated. With their last "thump," I finally snapped. I turned and smacked all three of them across their faces in one sweeping gesture.

They jumped me.

Leroy pulled the bus over.

Since I was white and Leroy was black, and I was the one caught "hitting," I expected to feel the full weight of his wrath. I just hoped he wouldn't hurt me too badly, because my head was still sore.

The girls looked smug. Their pressed hair was sticking up everywhere from the fight, incriminating me further.

Leroy said, "What happened here?"

"They wouldn't stop thumping me on the back of the head. I finally had to smack them to get it to stop."

"Nuh-uh," they chanted sweetly. One of them said, "She just smacked us for no reason."

Leroy grinned. It was the first time I'd seen his teeth all year. The white kids at our school didn't pick fights with the black kids. It's like a pygmy entering a boxing ring with a prizefighter. It doesn't happen. I expected Leroy to side with them anyway.

Instead he said, "You girls better keep your hands to yourself or you'll be dealing with me instead of her next time. Understand?"

Their half-jeering faces froze.

Then he made an announcement, "Don't let me catch y'all hitting anyone, ya hear? If someone hits you first, come get me."

I was surprised when he asked, "Are you okay?"

"Yes, sir." I said as I rubbed the back of my skull.

A fair, smart, competent adult connected to the public school system wasn't something I expected. On another day, Leroy helped me again. My neighbor Sonya wanted to fight me after school. She used to be my best friend, but she'd become conceited since joining the cheerleading squad. When she refused to play with me, I told her she needed a beating. I was thinking it should come from her Mom, but she invited me to give it to her instead. Some kids told me that she planned to have her brother join in the fight too, so I got off at a different bus stop.

As I walked away, Leroy slammed on the brakes and leapt off the bus. "They said this isn't your stop."

"No, it isn't. Sonya wants to fight, and she's having her brother jump in too."

"Get back on here, then."

I skulked up the steps.

Sonya's pig face glowered.

Leroy saw. He cocked his head to the side and pierced her with one menacing, brown eye, "Don't you be fighting after you get off this bus. If I hear anything about a fight, you'll be dealing with me tomorrow. Do ya hear?"

Her snotty expression crumpled.

I exhaled in relief.

Leroy saved other students from bullying that year, regardless of their ethnicity. He didn't have to stop the bus that day or intercede on our behalf. No one was watching except a bunch of kids. During a racially charged time in our city, Leroy didn't take his frustration out on us. I'm grateful for what he taught me even more than what he saved me from: Stand up for what is fair without partiality. Many people prefer not to get involved. I guess they didn't have a Leroy.

I sometimes still think about him. Was he was a good father, does he still live in Las Vegas, did he continue to drive a bus and protect children? What has become of him? I don't know. One thing I am sure of: in 1975 Las Vegas, a black bus driver named Leroy was one little girl's hero.

Roger A. Hanson, Ph.D.

Shelter Belts

On a Saturday morning in October, 1958, from the moment my eyes opened, I quickly dressed and then looked at myself in the mirror. I was a young hunter in brown shotgun shell vest, hat, pants, and a bright red long sleeve shirt. However, no gazing was allowed because I did not want to be late when Alan and Kevin arrived to pick me up for our trip to the heart of the pheasant country in North Dakota. My mother commented, "I haven't seen you this organized before."

Our hunting party actually grew out of competition with one another. Members of different neighborhood outdoor rink hockey teams, starting at the age of 10, we quickly became acquainted through regular Saturday morning city-wide youth league games. It's difficult not to know someone who body checks you into wooden boards causing you to fall down, takes the puck away, and then slaps it into your team's net for a goal. However, the speed and precision at which hockey is played, especially skating backward, induce an appreciation for athletic talent of others. Our team rivalries continued until we reached the same high school. Once on the same team, it didn't take too much time to bond and strengthen our growing friendship by common interests in golf.

Alan was the better athlete, first line center in hockey, and had been among the final four players in a national junior amateur golf tournament held in Seattle, Washington the previous summer. His two older brothers excelled at the same two sports and held the local golf courses' scoring records. Alan followed in this tradition, but he was regarded as even more promising. His potential was well recognized. The teaching professional at the local country club was a mentor; he regularly invited Alan to practice with him. In manners and social behavior, Alan showed the benefits of stable, closely knit family relationships. He was modest and well disciplined compared to Kevin and me. I respected him greatly, but I simultaneously enjoyed breaking rules myself.

When Alan asked me whether I wanted to join his father and him on a hunting trip, I immediately said, "Far out, you're damm right. It will be a helluva blast." His equally quick reaction was, "That's great, but you'll have to watch your language. My father takes church seriously." Grimacing, I promised to avoid any profanity—a small price to pay in exchange for a promise of a great time.

Kevin likely accepted Alan's offer just as quickly and gratefully. However, they probably enjoyed some humor at my expense when Alan said I also was a partner to the party. We had previously tried skeet shooting on two occasions. The results demonstrated clay pigeons were not in danger from me. Perhaps I led them too far or not far enough. Or maybe I flinched just before pulling the trigger. My skill or lack of it at a local gun club was consistent with my minimal success during our informal practice efforts shooting beer bottles and cans at a nearby quarry. When it was my turn, an object went up, and then it came down. No bottles burst in the air and no cans were blown away. Of course, Alan and Kevin did well at both the formal and informal arenas. Thankfully, they kept their ribbing to a minimum.

Thinking and preparing for the trip were done solitarily. Perhaps we had other friends and interests or maybe it was the thing to do, especially when we were just aspiring huntsmen. We had our own separate fantasies, or at least I did. My image of us at the end of the day was a magnificent display in the local newspaper of us with a maximum number of pheasants. I tried to keep my head attached to my body by concentrating attention on my gun and the appropriate shotgun shell to use. I told myself over and over again, we weren't going on an African safari in search of some rare or fearsome species. I simply wanted to avoid coming home empty handed. If I had known more at the time, I would have thought, "My goal is to avoid an ignominious ride home."

To save money, I had purchased my gun at Johnson's Sporting Good's huge arsenal the year before during the late off season at a relatively low price. Money earned from caddying during the summer enabled me to enjoy the pride of ownership. It was a 12 gauge pump action; by moving the gun handle or pump a spent shell could be ejected and another one reloaded quickly. This gauge had maximum power, and certainly my shoulder felt the recoil when the gun fired. The substantial weight of my gun made maneuvering a challenge, but I chose it also to hunt ducks that generally are more distant targets than pheasants. Additionally, since I planned using the gun for several years, I fully expected to become physically able to fire it more effectively.

The gun was important to me and represented a symbol of oncoming adulthood. I purchased it before being able to apply for an automobile driver's license, buy alcoholic beverages, or enlist in the armed forces. After regularly cleaning and oiling the barrel, I stored it on my highest bedroom shelf inaccessible to my 10 year old sister. I polished the stock and barrel the night before our trip and gently put the gun back in its special place.

Concerning the shotgun shells, I went back and forth up to the day before the trip on what "number" or shot size to use. There was a range of options from number 2 to number 9 and having options made me want to choose the perfect alternative instead of simply choosing an appropriate one. Ringing loudly, the last bell on Friday signaled the end of classes for the week and the necessity of making a decision. Off to Johnson's Sporting Goods store I went. Deliberatively assessing shot size had become part of a ritual in my mind. The store's displays provided practical help by making available easy to understand, relevant, written guidelines on this matter. Yet, the preferred alternative still did come to me.

What grabbed my attention was a cool, open cross section of a shotgun shell mounted on a store counter revealing what the inside of a shell looked like. There was primer consisting of chemicals that exploded when the trigger was pulled and the gun's firing pin hit the primer; powder that burned after the primer's explosion forming gases which pushed the shot out of the barrel; wad paper that helped keep the shot together as it left the barrel of the gun; and shot, small pieces of metal in the form of BBs. I must have stared at this single exposed shell for a long time. The clerk finally asked me, "Are you going to make a purchase or are you here to write a paper?" I meekly said, "I'm a buyer," in the same tone of voice as if I had asked, "More gruel, sir?"

My problem was not a failure to recognize basic differences between shot sizes. It was established that the smaller the number of the shot, the larger the size of the metal discharges and the tighter their cluster after firing. What made the decision hard for me was that it required taking both a gun's gauge and the nature of the target into account. Large projectiles fired from a 12 gauge gun, which had maximum power, might brutally rip a pheasant apart leaving very little meat to eat. I agonizingly narrowed down the alternatives, after another half an hour of scrutiny, to 6 or 71/2 shot. When the clerk came by again, I impulsively said, "Two boxes of 71/2 shells, please." Apparently I had flipped a coin in my mind and 71/2 came up on the right side.

From the sporting goods shop, I went to a movie, *The Young Lions*, starring Marlon Brando, Montgomery Clift, and Dean Martin. After the night out, it was homeward bound for some shuteye. I didn't count pheasants before nodding off; sleep was made easy by the prospect of a totally pleasant Saturday.

Since none of us yet owned our own car, the expedition was made possible by Alan's father's willingness to take us with him. On entering the car, I saw the father's shotgun that resembled a canon with a silver colored barrel, two inches longer than ours. Alan said, "It's a goose gun." Alan's own gun was a pump action like mine, and Kevin's was a single shot; he would have to crack the gun barrel from the stock and manually reload after every firing.

The spectacular history of where we lived contributed to a particular perspective that I carried even on the trip. The last Ice Age occurred here thousands of years ago, and the melting glaciers formed a gigantic body of water ultimately named Lake Agassiz. This Lake contained more water than all of the lakes in the modern world. Silt from the lake bottom made the soil in this part of the country extremely rich and fertile for crops pheasants thrive on. And we all had attended Agassiz Junior High School.

The direct line I saw from geological formations 30,000 years ago to the name of our school coincided with a personal perspective. I seemed to move from one scrape to another without damaging myself irreparably. Yes, I was disciplined, honors were denied or even taken away; I failed when I should have succeeded, and at times I was shunned. Despite my follies and lack of sensibility, I managed to avoid catastrophe and occasionally got ahead a bit. Hence, I was emerging oddly with a fairly sunny outlook, which probably accounted for my expectations in bagging something on our trip even if it was the pheasant's little cousin, the partridge. They were abundant and more importantly flew close together. How could I miss?

However, zany teenage theorizing about my fate in life did not inhibit or suppress my excitement and anticipation over what was right in front of me. We lived only two hours away from the hunting area. Normally, to pass the time we would have engaged in bathroom jokes and flatulent competitions during the ride, if it had occurred on a school bus. The presence of Alan's father banished such conversation. My limited good sense prevailed and I kept lewd thoughts to myself. To fill this void, I was made the butt of dumb comments about my hunting skills.

"So the boys tell me you're quite a marksman," Alan's father innocently said to me. Before I could utter a response, Kevin commented, "That's right, only it's spelled 'Marx-man'." They joyfully said together, "He isn't used to the over and under feature of his gun and that's why he is over sometimes and under other times." I cringed because their claims were true, not because of their dumb, juvenile nature. Yet, this day promised to be different.

Alan's father was taking us to a prime location he favored. His character and beliefs on how things should be done were palpable. He exuded wisdom concerning the ways of pheasants; where they eat, sleep and luxuriate. His tan face and solemnity made me think he was a seasoned guide charting a course in the right direction at the right time. We were on our way to Lindenwood, a town appropriately named since it was one of the few places where trees grew in some abundance. As Alan's father explained, "Trees are important to us. Pheasants hide out comfortably in shelter belts."

Shelter belts are planned resistance to the winds of the prairie threatening to damage crops and erode the soil. The belts tend to be bordered by un-kept sprawling trees and densely covered in-between with thick brush, wild flowers, weeds and whatever else nature allows to grow. Trees grow at sharp angles reflecting the strong winds blowing across the fields. The ground between the two rows of trees is not maintained, and uneven with holes here and there. On the flat prairie, shelter belts stand out. They run perpendicular to roads or are planted a considerable distance away from roads and deep into farm lands. Either way, you have to walk in and then walk out. As a result, I learned hunting is hard work. Plowing through underbrush for a quarter of a mile is tough, prickly and hot. And repeating this exercise across multiple shelter belts is exhausting.

The most common alternative to trekking through shelter belts is to walk through rows of long corn fields. Certainly pheasants are present in these feeding areas. However, the length of the fields made it possible for different groups of hunters unknowingly to enter opposite ends, proceed to walk towards each other and thereby unintentionally fire in the direction of the other group. One of my cousins had almost lost an eye the previous year when hit in this manner. Even more risky was the practice of shooting at pheasants from inside a car. Pheasants tend to ingest small stones into their gullets for digestive purposes at the end of the day. They find the stones on gravel roads. In response, some hunters drive at sunset looking for birds in roadside ditches and prepare to shoot them through open windows. Of course, if ambushed, pheasants fly back across a road instead of directly away from it creating the obvious hazard of guns being fired by passengers in awkward positions and possibly in the direction of oncoming vehicles. In addition, hunters might be leaving corn fields just as someone in a car begins shooting at a pheasant flushed from the roadside in the direction of the field. What we were doing seemed both relatively safe and salutary.

Nevertheless, when we broke for lunch my pouch was still empty, Alan's father was at his limit, and Alan and Kevin each had one under their belts. The shells on my hunting vest seemed especially heavy, not because of their physical weight, but because they had the character of fatuous decorations rather than a hunter's tools. However, I did share fatigue with my friends; the three of us were bushed while Alan's father appeared to enjoy the terrain and took in the day for what it was intended, a break from traditional Saturday chores. I wished I knew how he knew where and how to walk so deftly.

After lunch, we headed out to find promising pheasant havens. As we drove onward, geese were flying sky high because of the fair weather. No sense in trying to surprise ducks in a slough, because they likely were joining their feathered friends in atmospheric altitudes. So we had to find fowl in the thickets.

Our next stop required a walk to the end of a belt about a quarter of a mile away from the road where we parked the car. So the plan was to walk to the far end of the shelter belt and return walking four abreast back to the county road. During the morning I had noticed Alan's father watching me. He surely saw my nervous reactions when birds fluttered up and my failures to shoot when I intended to because I had failed to switch off the safety switch. Instead of giving me a lecture, Alan's father respectively looked at me and reminded me of the most essential precepts, "Relax, take your time, and squeeze, don't pull the trigger." He was continuing to hunt and generously offering pheasants he bagged to any of us who might be under the limit. I liked him more and more.

We marched in. Reaching the far end first, I had a decision to make. Since the custom was for Alan's father to take a position close to the trees on the near outside of the belt, I went forward expecting to take a position at the center. However, the entrance to the middle of the belt was grossly overgrown and had probably been filled with water in the spring. Instead of weeds, cattails, and other wild plants and brush being knee high or waist high, they were shoulder high and thick with thistles. God help me I thought and I said, "Jesus, this is a jungle, not hunter's heaven." Alan responded to my remark and said, "Watch it. Cool down. Remember my dad."

I chose to go to the far edge of the belt near the other line of trees expecting to find an easier pathway. I was uninterested in surprising birds when I couldn't see where I was going. Of course, my decision meant Alan and Kevin had to work the center. Because the middle portion of the belt was so overgrown, Alan went first and then Kevin followed closely behind; they entered in a single file line in search of more feasible, separate paths.

Within 30 seconds after we began walking, I heard a gun shot, but didn't see any startled birds fly up and away. Instead, a horrible accident had occurred. Alan had been shot in the back. Kevin's gun had discharged at point blank range. The entire wad and shot projectiles from Kevin's shotgun shell had gone into Alan's back cavity. I saw Alan flailing wildly on the ground, screaming in intense pain. He was several yards from his father and me. When we reached him, blood was not splattered. The wound was deep inside.

We managed to carry Alan back to the car and then drove to the hospital in Lindenwood. During the entire ride, no one spoke. Kevin's pale face simply stared out the front window, not looking at anyone. Alan's father did all he could do to keep the car on the road at its maximum speed while thinking about the condition of the youngest of his three sons. I silently sat in the back seat holding Alan, who was stretched out. I didn't know what to do. None of us acted as if we were alive. The only sound was Alan's moaning, until he too was quiet and no longer trembled. I knew he was dying in my arms. Emergency room treatment was essential. He was pronounced dead shortly on arrival.

The transformation from the awful sounds of gun fire, pain and road noise to silence within the car was accompanied by a change in color. The day had been blessed with a bright sun, clear sky and multicolored pheasants; they had green heads, red wattles, white neck circles, and long black tails. Even the brown clothing all around was eye catching. In sharp contrast, the colors in the car now were gray and black. The sky suddenly was overcast, the temperature dropping, the clothing faded into an indistinguishable color, and the car's interior seemed completely dull. Perhaps reality didn't change, but my perceptions certainly did.

The sudden coldness of the afternoon coincided with the abrupt realization of the inherent remoteness of the shelter belt and its consequences. It became clear once we were at the hospital; there was no way we could have saved Alan. Carrying Alan from the field to the car was time consuming. Even if we had been roadside at the point of the accident we couldn't have taken him to the hospital in a few minutes, no matter how fast we drove. Distance can't be shortened. A sense of hopelessness made me feel numb all over.

The return car ride home was excruciatingly sorrowful, no explanations, excuses, or exclamations. There was only bitter silence. Our goodbyes to each other were mute. That evening a newspaper reporter called me for an account of what had happened. Alan's parents would only have time to grieve privately until Sunday morning when the death of their son was front page news. I mumbled something to the reporter, hung up and looked to my mother for understanding.

The cause of the accident, if there is one, was not the subject of discussion on that day, or any day since, as far as I know. Possibly branches pulled back the trigger of Kevin's gun. Or Kevin might have stumbled and his hand slipped and hit the triggering mechanisms. Maybe the gun already was cocked to permit reloading as quickly as possible. Was my decision to avoid the middle of the belt the underlying cause? Can it be blamed on shelter belts?

The tragedy's complexities swamped attempts retrospectively to sort out a precise account of what happened. When real events happen without the clarity of deliberate intent or conscious control, their speed is frighteningly faster and in unexpected directions, they are more dramatic than creative fiction. Dreams and nightmares distort recollections. Consequently, un-testable assumptions have to be made to reconstruct reality, because memories are murky and thereby make conclusions intrinsically unreliable.

Calamities' participants do not sit down and dispassionately debrief expert analysts as supposedly is the case in highly planned law enforcement or military operations. The only comfortable opportunity I had to unburden myself was when my favorite teacher asked me after class on Monday, "What the hell happened?" He was understanding and sympathetic; Alan and I were students in the same course. All that we knew with certainty was that there had been a tragedy. Unfortunately, grief counseling and trauma therapy were far less common then as they are today.

Later that fall, I was cruising Johnson's Sporting Goods for hockey skates. Once again, I walked by the used gun supply. There for sale was a long, silver barreled goose gun. It unmistakably had belonged to Alan's father. The season was over forever.

Cindy Warren

Walking with Buddha

I like to meditate. Well, I'm trying to like it anyway. Like exercise, it always feels better after I'm through. Tonight, I'm driving to a Buddhist meditation class. The forty-minute drive is spent dreaming about golden statues and lavish gardens tended by illuminated monks, whose holy devotion can lift mere mortals like me to ascetic states of contemplation and enlightenment, where a kaleidoscope of beauty is nurtured by hands more holy—those metta-sending deliverers of loving-kindness. I'm more like a mud-basking hippopotamus, partially submerged, meditating horizontally in my tub.

Most of my life I spent talking to whoever crossed my path. Lately, I've been thinking that I'd like to become a better listener, both in my personal and spiritual life. It seems like the first step would be to sit down and shut up, so I locate a Buddhist Temple on Meet-up.com. The website says that tonight's lesson is on three types of Buddhist meditation, if I can just get there. MapQuest leads me to a run-down, but busy side street. Making a left at a sterile, white meeting hall, I see no grass, much less a garden.

Cars zip through the parking lot using it as a thoroughfare between two streets. A white Honda almost strikes a teenager on a ten-speed. He appears unfazed, so I call out from my parked car, "Is this the Buddhist Temple?"

He pedals away from me faster and says, "I dunno."

As I get out of my car, a man in a pin-stripe suit rushes toward a side door. I accost him, "Is this the 7:00 p.m. meditation?"

Ignoring me, he flees into the building. Perhaps the monk-in-charge can send him some loving-kindness, because it won't be coming from me. I get back in, slam my car door shut, and speed out of the parking lot. Across the street, there are several parked cars lined up along the side of the road. A man in sweats is sprinting toward an old ranch style house. It's 7:05 and I'm late. I roll down the window and wince. "Is there a meditation here?"

He nods yes before escaping inside.

Approaching the dilapidated house is disappointing. I am expecting a lavish temple. Dozens of shoes line the area around an open door, including a diseased pair of green flip-flops that even Goodwill would be afraid to handle. As my former visions of Eastern grandeur deflate, I have a fleeting impulse to run. My curiosity, however, propels me over the threshold.

A dozen giant, pink floor pillows are spaced along a dimly lit rectangle that was once somebody's living room. As I enter, I smile and try to make eye contact with people already seated in the cross-legged position, but they aren't having it. A handsome, forty-year-old man in jeans is speaking in a low, flat monotone, "The small one-foot cushion is for elevating the hips and aligning the spine." Nobody has acknowledged the lone, frenetic stranger whose popping knees perforate the silence.

At the front of the room sits a giant, unsmiling, ivory Buddha elevated precariously on a folding table. He's five feet tall and just as wide. I can't take my eyes off him. A candle flickers in a hurricane lamp. I breathe in the spicy aroma of something like frankincense. They also have an altar set up with several smaller Buddhas interspersed around it. Just as Christ had the twelve disciples, it appears that big Buddha has little Buddhas.

The speaker introduces the three types of meditation: concentration, mindfulness, and metta. "Metta is the act of sending out loving-kindness, and we must start by sending it to ourselves." The fat statue is distracting. *Did he say mindfulness or concentration is about paying attention to the breath?* Tucking my feet in a modified lotus position, I wish I'd worn socks. I'm self-conscious about having my unpainted toes examined by unsmiling strangers. He continues, "Non-attachment is neither being excited by good news nor disappointed by bad."

I figure this might happen once I've stopped breathing.

Quieting my mind is especially difficult around so many new people. I breathe in and out, trying to halt my racing thoughts. *Is the absence of Buddha's jolly smile because he's non-attached? Is the speaker saying I'm not supposed to be happy, like the statue?* Finally, I tell myself "stop." The mental chatter subsides. When a random thought invades, I "halt" it. After about fifteen minutes, I open my eyes and look at big Buddha. I think of him and Jesus, both great teachers and wise men. I ask them, God, the angels—whoever is listening—*help me make sense of these two incongruent teachings: how do I reconcile the Buddhist practice of non-attachment with the*

Christian teaching to rejoice always? Closing my eyes, I draw in a long slow breath. Finally, a flash of insight emerges; embrace both. Isn't it possible that both Jesus and Buddha can be right?

For someone who likes to sit in silence for several hours each day, it's surprising that our teacher is still talking. "I meditate a minimum of two hours each morning and each evening," he says, looking pleased with himself. He's become almost animated, "We can't get away from people, and that's just the way it is." His intolerance crashes through the spicy air. We hold our breath in disbelief. As someone he can't escape, I imagine his disdain for a noisy, renegade, thirty-minute meditator like me.

To the teacher's right is a *real* Buddhist, a bald-headed young monk wearing an orange robe. I'd prefer to have someone well-decorated teaching me, but I'm stuck with the guy in jeans that doesn't like people. Directed to begin a thirty-minute sitting meditation, he encourages us to try metta, mindfulness, or concentration. Everyone closes their eyes but me. I'm curious about these flaccid souls. I routinely examine them when I should be practicing. They seem peaceful, but not happy. I guess that's what happens when you aren't allowed to get too excited about anything. To their credit, they have held the cross-legged lotus position all night without so much as a twitch, while I fidget more than a five-year-old.

As the speaker reminds us to pay attention to the breath, I get a cramp. I gingerly uncross my legs and shake them out, hoping nobody hears. The small pillow under my tailbone has become stuck. I dig it out and stick it under one knee, like our speaker. The sound of it slapping the immaculate wood floor makes me cringe. He mentioned earlier that he has a knee problem. I don't, but the pillow feels a damn site better there than it did wedged under my coccyx. I wish I had one for the other leg.

Thirty minutes later, a Tibetan singing bowl sounds a few sweet notes signifying our transition to the walking meditation outside. Remembering the decaying flip-flops, I quickly grab my shoes lest someone decide to trade up. Relieved by the brief reprieve from silence, I stomp off to my place in line. It's dark. I'm not all that coordinated in daylight. Within seconds, I stumble into a gopher hole. The pious speaker is walking next to me and doesn't check to see if I broke anything. He seems to scoot over so I don't land on top of him. Rebalancing myself, I send him thoughts of loving-kindness, determined to take a step toward the light.

We put one foot in front of the other, stop, meditate, repeat. A crisp, southwestern breeze wafts by as I ponder what I've been taught. I concentrate harder to quiet my galloping thoughts. Walk, stop, breathe, meditate. Watch for gopher holes. When I turn around at the rickety old fence, the heavenly glow of a bright yellow, full moon bursts down upon me. It illuminates the twinkling cerulean-cobalt sky and fills me with joy. While this wasn't the enchanted evening of my fantasies, I'm delighted to have learned more about how to meditate, and for the knowledge of how to reconcile the teachings of Jesus and Buddha. But, perhaps most of all, I'm happy to report that I have a strong preference for my tub.

Loren Stephens

Singing the Praises of LINGO1

Forget auras and ESP. Forget consulting psychics who hand out advice to the lovelorn, seekers of the truth, first-time home buyers, or fearful investors who don't know if we are heading for inflation or deflation, a bull or bear market. Leave it up to your essential familial tremor, if you are lucky enough to have one.

Although I haven't checked the statistics, I could fall back on the "10% theory" which estimates that 10% of Americans have some form of addiction, or are currently under-employed, or are dissatisfied with their sex life. So let's just say that as many as 10% of Americans have essential familial tremor. I am among this select cohort.

You might have noticed someone standing in line at the bank, or perhaps at the supermarket, with a head that shakes slightly, or you might be sitting next to someone at a concert whose program rustles like leaves in the autumn breeze because their hand cannot hold steady. These might just be essential familial tremors.

Just in case you think that essential familial tremor is below the radar, think again. There is an International Essential Familial Tremor Association whose slogan is, "A single voice is seldom heard but a thousand voices shake the world."

My tremor is restricted to my head—a slightly perceptible shaking from side to side that is exacerbated by caffeine, nervous tension (what medical condition, isn't?), staring at the computer for long hours, losing satellite connection on my GPS on a lonely dark road at midnight. It is at its most noticeable when I am confronted with a proposition with which I am uncomfortable—let's say being asked to co-sign a mortgage for a friend, or lending money without the promise of repayment—or if I meet someone who gives off what I call toxicity. Then my head starts to shake, which can be uncomfortable not only for me, but for the person who is looking at me. And that is when I ask myself, *Why am I having this reaction? Why is my tremor being stirred up? What is it about this person, this situation, that is not healthy for me?*

In the past, I chalked these incidences up to nerves, but over time I have recognized that my essential familial tremor is trying to tell me something, which is why I say, "Forget about ESP, psychics." I rely on my tremor to give me critical clues that will help me make important decisions. I have learned to embrace what I viewed in the past as an annoyance at best and an embarrassment at worst.

My tremor became noticeable when I was in my mid-fifties. I thought it was caused by a neck injury from a car accident at age fifteen. I suffered a concussion, was in a coma for twenty-four hours, and had a broken nose as a souvenir. My neck muscles were compromised, and years later, I developed neck pain and muscle weakness. To add insult to injury, in my late forties I discovered a lump in my neck that turned out to be a parotid tumor of the salivary gland, requiring a seven-hour surgery to remove the benign growth. I have scar tissue down my neck which occasionally pulls so hard it has a lively conversation with my tremor, thus irritating my condition.

I consulted Dr. Andrew Woo, a specialist at Saint John's Hospital and Medical Center in Santa Monica, who gave me a neurological workup and took my family history, which was illuminating. Strange that I never connected the dots, but I consider myself blessed with excellent health and don't look for trouble, especially of the hereditary kind, because what can you do about it anyway? For instance, I have no interest in finding out if I have a propensity for cancer. It is not something that ever crosses my mind. I ascribe to the school of "To think is to create," and therefore the last thing I want to think about is cancer.

Dr. Woo examined me, asking me to touch my nose with my eyes closed, draw a spiral, and sign my name on a piece of paper. He checked my reflexes with a rubber hammer, and my legs and arms happily jerked to meet his gaze. He then asked me, "Has anyone in your family had Parkinson's disease?"

"Yes, my great-grandmother, Bella Unterberg."

"What about your grandmother?"

"Well, she had *grand mal* seizures. Didn't help her disposition any." Dr. Woo laughed.

"And what about your mother?"

"She had a minor head tremor, which also manifested itself in a slight lip quiver, but it never seemed to bother her."

"And are each of these women the first-born of their generation?"

"Yes, and so am I."

So it seems that *familial* is the operative term in the case of my tremor, targeting female first-borns in our family. It is an inherited trait, and based upon a study at Beth Israel Hospital in New York (where I agreed to participate in a blind study), it most often shows itself among Ashkenazi Jews with roots in Eastern Europe and Russia. My mother's family emigrated from Poland in the early nineteenth century, and among the personal effects they brought with them might have been "LINGO1," the gene that is tentatively attributed to essential familial tremor. The Beth Israel study also finds that essential familial tremor shows itself more frequently than might be expected among Mennonites. Are they also the chosen people? Originally persecuted Anabaptists, they escaped to Holland and Germany, and eventually came to the United States. I am proud to say that they are a peace-loving people. Some Mennonites still drive around in horse-and-buggy and have no use for GPS systems, which is not a problem when they have essential familial tremors to point them in the right and righteous direction.

Essential familial tremors exist on a continuum from mild to severe, with treatment prescribed according to the severity of the tremor. I am one of the lucky among the 10%ers with a very mild tremor.

Dr. Woo prescribed a minimum dose of clonazepam, which belongs to a group of drugs called benzodiazepines. These drugs block the effects of a specific chemical involved in the transmission of impulses in the brain, decreasing the excitement levels of the nerve cells. There is some debate about whether the tremor is caused by the firing of nerve endings which agitate the brain's chemistry, or vice versa. It's sort of a chicken-and-egg argument, but suffice it to say, the stuff works. Once you get on the right dosage, you don't want to go cold turkey or forget to take the medication. I won't go into the potential calamities that might occur. If you are really curious about the drug's potency, there is always Google, but I'd rather rely on those little contraindication printouts and label warnings on the medicine bottle, and leave it at that as in, "Don't operate heavy machinery until you have adjusted to this medication; may cause drowsiness; avoid alcohol." That last one is harsh since—through trial and error—I have discovered that a few sips of champagne have a calming effect on my tremor.

Dr. Woo recommended physical exercise to strengthen muscles and release tension (good for an active sex life, too), massage (same), and anything else that diffuses tension in the body and raises endorphin levels, which are the source of happiness and health.

On my own, I discovered the therapeutic benefits of singing. Every Wednesday morning for a half an hour, I take lessons at Carol Tingle's cozy studio in Santa Monica. Climbing the stairs, I let go of my to-do list, quiet my monkey brain that swings among the tortured vines of obligations and annoyance, and picture myself on stage at the Gardenia, an intimate cabaret in West Hollywood where I will have my imagined singing debut.

Every lesson begins with a warm-up: first, scales to exercise my head voice, a place where sopranos feel comfortable, and then, I drop down into my chest voice. That is where I often end up with the croakies, half-human, half-beast sounds that Carrie makes in the Stephen King horror movie of the same name. If I am tired, if I have breathed in too much of LA's dust, or the air is dry, if I have had milk with my heart-healthy cereal, it all shows up.

Right now I am working on "I Got Lost In His Arms" from Irving Berlin's *Annie Get Your Gun*. I brave the low notes and whisper some of the lyrics to convey the feelings of a woman who accidentally finds love, lets go of all her lifelines, and succumbs to the magic of a man *Whose arms held me fast/and broke the fall*. And what is remarkable is that my head is as steady as a rock while I am singing, at least in the safety of Carol Tingle's studio.

After three years of lessons, I decided to audition for cabaret camp. Although I had no illusions that I was headed for a career in cabaret any time soon, I relished the idea of spending a week in the Colorado Rockies (think of Maria in *The Sound of Music* warbling, "The hills are alive. . .") with aspiring singers and a teaching staff of well-known cabaret artists and their pianists. This was a "no kidding" workshop in which semiprofessional students were expected to leave with a polished act they could take on the road. What was I thinking? I was in way over my head.

I arrived at the audition with two songs—my standby, "Lost in His Arms," and "Autumn Leaves." The pianist smiled reassuringly as he set my music down on his white, baby grand piano. Miss C., who is the leading lady of cabaret, sat on a sofa opposite me and just stared.

My head started to shake uncontrollably, although I had taken an extra dose of clonazepam just for safety's sake. I tried calming my nerves by reminding myself, *This is only for fun, and you know her. Back in the day when you were a theater producer you even auditioned her. You have hired her. Get a grip.* But my self-talk was of no use. Without smiling, or any acknowledgment that we had a prior relationship, Miss C. asked, "So what are you going to sing for us?"

"Autumn Leaves."

"One of my favorites. I have performed it many times. Delicious." And then she burrowed down into the cushions on the sofa and waited, like a lioness licking her chops.

The music started. My voice sounded like it belonged to someone else. Where had all the training gone? I rushed the vowels and headed straight for the sand traps of "t," "w," and "d." I tried a few hand gestures, pointing out the window on the words "the autumn leaves drift by my window." It was utterly humiliating, and there was nowhere to run, nowhere to hide. Mercifully, she cut me off mid-lyric.

"Well, I think we have heard enough." And then she addressed the pianist as if I was invisible, "You know, her voice sounds a bit like my mother's when she's clearing her throat." She then did a convincing imitation of a consumptive.

She leaned toward me, "Flat too. Come back next year."

I gathered up my music—no point in singing "I Got Lost in His Arms." I was done for. I whispered "thank you" and left. I sat in my car. I looked like one of those bobble dolls in the back window of a low rider. Once I got my bearings, I realized my essential familial tremor was telegraphing "Toxic, toxic" like a blinking light at a railroad crossing warning drivers of an oncoming train.

I received a call the next day from the pianist offering me a place in cabaret camp. He explained, "Without your tuition, there won't be enough students to amortize the cost of all the master teachers, so Miss C. changed her mind." He couldn't see me, but I deliberately turned my head to the left and right and answered, "No thank you."

THE END

Timothy L. Marsh

Patience

In the great routework of western America, there is not a single interstate bloodier or more carcass-décored than Interstate 90. One cannot drive a quarter mile along its pavement without having to swerve around or tread across the spilled, splattered, decimated remains of one animal or another, omnivore or carnivore, domesticated or feral. Steers, cows, dogs, deer, rabbits, possums, squirrels, foxes, coyotes, cats, bears—if a species makes its home in Big Sky country you can be sure you'll find a few of its members thoroughly mashed of life on the I-90.

I have always been inordinately intrigued by roadkill. I once counted fifty-seven on a dull stretch of I-5 just west of Mt. Shasta, including a black bear poised in full attack position, jaws wide open, front paws reaching out, its rigor mortis so posed and perfectly convincing that I was sure some taxidermist had lost something off the back of his truck. I pulled finders-keepers to the shoulder, imagining how cool my apartment would seem with a stuffed bear propped by the door for visitors to hang their coats on and pretend to battle or hump when they were drunk, only to find the bear rotted through the mouth with flies, its head screwed on sideways, the near-sure upshot of a midnight mauling by some beastly eighteen-wheeler.

Another time on my way to Bozeman I hit a bobcat dead on, veered to a halt and saw it scrambling in a tight circle on the shoulder of the road. The cat had hurled itself across my fender and detonated meteor-like upon impact. Its pain was astounding—the kind of anguish you can't turn your back on though you desperately want to, since it belongs to an injury miles beyond your ability to handle.

The animal will to survive can make a terrible maze of their final moments. There is no way of telling how much time it will take them to find the way to death, even if the wound is horrific. With that in mind I took the only blunt force object in my car, a 29-inch aluminum softball bat, and beat its skull to pieces in a roadside gully, because its back was broken and its hind legs were shattered and ripped from its body.

The cat knew what was happening and snarled and somehow juked my first two strikes before I landed the third, stunning it momentarily while I cocked back and delivered the hammer stroke, likely the fatal blow, though I struck it several times more to ensure my humaneness. After it was done I rolled the bat in some brush to wipe the mess off the barrel, little white bubbles blistering in the wound slurry that was now the bobcat's face.

It took about ten minutes to track the desperate animal and unleash my mercy. By the time I climbed out of the gully a single-column convoy of flatbed trucks had begun to seep down the highway, each truck lugging a cylindrical cask of nuclear waste, each cask apocalyptically decaled with a screaming emaciated skull like something from a Holocaust atrocity.

I must've been one hell of a rustic horror standing on the side of that highway holding a murder-smirched aluminum bat, the truly creepy prairie barrens of eastern Montana surging infinitely around me; but the procession never batted a brake light. The trucks filed by with the steady grim severity of a single bead of blood, owning nothing in their manner of transit that suggested the slightest concern for the peripheral world.

Even in the wake of what had just happened it was a sight to stop and watch, the rank-and-file of a dozen nuclear transports forming a kind of toxic-death slideshow, keeping strict procedural spacing from one another as they sought the opposite distance and then finally disappeared over a hill in the highway.

When the last truck was out of sight I washed my hands with some bottled water, used the rest to rinse the cat-smack off the fender, and got back on the road to Bozeman, where I spent the night slow-boozing in a low-country confederate pub boasting "Nuke Islam" bumper stickers above every urinal in the bathroom, pretty little mushroom clouds for exclamation points.

Thinking about that bobcat sometimes, or that bear, or the etcetera of simple instinct smeared across the world's highways, I cannot help but pity the wisdom of animals. They have not learned that the world is not theirs anymore, or that it could be again if they just stick to the hills a little while longer, away from the roads, and let us do our thing.

Michael Milburn

Thoughts On Life Span

> *Waiting for the end, boys, waiting for the end.*
> *What is there to be or do?*
> —William Empson

I trace the start of my preoccupation with mortality to the year 2000, when my father died at age eighty-two. Two years later I turned forty-five, and the combination of these events—my first significant death and arrival at middle age—left me in a permanent state of worry about life squandered and life slipping away. Since then, my fear of the future has not been dread of pain, debility, or no longer existing, but panic at having so little time. Time for what, I don't know. I tend to wish my days would pass more quickly, hurrying me to the week-end, vacation, a warmer or cooler season, the next promising experience, book, movie, CD.

Yet if I were given six months to live, I can't think what I would do differently from what I'm doing now. To some extent, I already live as if condemned—I try to minimize the amount of distracting (alas, paying) work that I do, thereby maximizing my time for things that are important to me like writing, and I tend to my relationships in part out of fear that I will one day look back and regret neglecting them. In both of these areas, I'm motivated by an awareness of life's brevity. Yet, as constructive as these attentions are, I would also love to forget about my impending death and enjoy the present. But how does someone my age—fifty-three—ignore the clock winding down, the finish line in view? Contemplating my middle-aged peers, I hear Philip Larkin's question about the elderly: "Why aren't they screaming?"

Presented with the six-month countdown, many people would choose to travel. I'm a cranky traveler, and anyway, what's the point? To take in as many new sights as possible before the end? I see no reason to stock up on memories if I'm going to die. If carpe diem is the plan, why not just increase my helping of the pleasures at hand—eating, drinking, smoking, sleeping late? I might spend extra quality time with my loved ones, but is life best savored by being concentrated into something unlike one's life—in my case, pumped full of company and new experiences? Besides, if my loved ones are such a priority or there's relationship building or repairing to do, why wait until I'm dying—why not act now?

There would appear to be something ill-conceived about our approach to the human life span if we start eyeing its end midway through. Half a life is a long time to spend waiting for a life to run down. It's not the total of years that bothers me, but knowing that there are fewer ahead than behind. Assured the longevity of Hanako, a koi who lived for 226 years, I could wait until age 113 to start fretting about my mortality; people cut down in their twenties may never feel finite at all. The current life expectancy for American males (77.5 years) looks generous or skimpy depending on one's perspective—infinite to a third grader, small change to the guy turning seventy-seven.

From my present vantage, my twenties are so indistinct they could have belonged to a different person. The decade they occupied, 1977-87, flickers in my mind like a nostalgic VH1 documentary—Ronald Reagan, disco, and Dallas. As for my thirties and forties, if not for photographs and my vivid twenty-four year old son, I would doubt I had lived through them at all. Which leaves me only a few more decades until my whole life will seem to have passed in an eye blink. Perhaps my inclination to brood over these late years will preserve them better than my overlooked youth—"We feel our lives most when they are running out," the novelist David Grossman wrote. Inconveniently, the particulars of my life right now are less salient than ever before. For example, I spent Christmas Eve 1980 snowbound in a hut in Finnish Lapland, whereas my last seven Christmases took place in the same house on the same suburban Connecticut street with the same people and the same plastic tree—hardly the stuff of colorful deathbed reminiscences.

I don't mean to sound valedictory. People born before me are considered youthful in many cultures and contexts. The only thing that makes me feel mortal is my obsession with my mortality. Chronologically speaking, I'm like a sailor just past the midpoint of an ocean crossing, with open water ahead and behind, tired from the trip but still a long way from landfall. Looked at this way, the human life span is just right; if one lives out one's projected days, one will have had one's chances—to screw up and rebound, to be precocious, to develop slowly and blossom late. There's time for everything and then some. In fact, I'm often amazed by how long life is, long enough that I can walk into a classroom and hear a computer programmed by my students wish me good morning, then read in that same day's newspaper a letter from a woman arrested in 1936 for conspiring to kill Stalin.

My mother was forty-six when I was born; four years later she suffered a stroke that impaired her hearing and equilibrium for the rest of her life. I think of her has having had two lives. By the time of her stroke, she had enjoyed as many healthy years as I have now been alive. For the next four decades, which supply all my memories of her, she was chronically dizzy and tired, conducting much of her family and social life from her bed. She died when I was forty-seven, an age at which she had almost half her life ahead of her. At her funeral, it occurred to me that I might be embarking on my own second act, free of the naiveté of youth. Yet all I could think was that with nearly half a century under my belt, my time was running out.

It's not just worrying about mortality that wastes my time, but worrying about worrying about it. I envy people my age who just plain live. But if they aren't thinking about the transience of their lives, aren't they sort of squandering them? Can one take full advantage of an opportunity if one does not acknowledge it as such? Carefree people get on my nerves, though it's my lack of this quality that keeps me from enjoying life. Whenever I try to savor a moment, it's immediately overrun by anxieties: Vacation ends tomorrow! Did I leave the stove on? Is my companion unhappy? Maybe life, for some, is meant to be just o. k., like a warm bath that never gets hot enough to be truly pleasurable.

When I hear the term "life span," I think of a bridge arching over a body of water, or an outspread hand used as a unit of measurement, precise in the sense that the fingers can only reach so far. I'm reminded of how worn my father's teeth looked on his deathbed, as if manufactured to last the length of a human life and no longer. Though the word "span" implies fixity, when applied to a life, it varies according to longevity and the point from which we contemplate it. As the amount of time behind and ahead of us changes, so does our sense of time wasted (or fulfilled) and running out (or available). Both portions look different at different ages— until I turned forty my future shimmered ahead with the abundance of a million dollar bank heist of which I'd only spent $500 on a new TV so far.

Technically, a life span connects birth to death, representing the transit of someone who has died. Maybe my obsessing about mortality is an attempt to gauge the length of mine before it has reached its opposite shore. If I could just desist from measuring, and focus on what fulfills me now, I'd accrue a span to be proud of. As for the spans of others, I think of my son's as a quarter of the way along, still rising and reaching, with the cresting and descending rest of it filled in by my own experience. So much of what I think about and say to him is based on this projection of his future, as I predict what he will eventually know, feel, want, or wish he had done. Mostly I envision the arc of peoples' lives according to the seventy odd years average, but when my former student died at twenty-four, it turned out my imagery was all off—Jon's midpoint was back *there*, his college years not prelude but denouement. I pictured an arch truncated, abandoned, its funding withdrawn.

Although my father's dates are long fixed (1917-2000), my perception of what lies between them keeps changing as my memory remixes his life. Gradually, though, his span is becoming a solid bar for me to caress, kick at, hang from, slither up and off like a greased pole. I wish I'd had more of this span-sense when he was alive, but he was too much a part of my forging of my own life for me to have perspective on his. Saul Bellow wrote, "Losing a parent is something like driving through a plate glass window. You didn't know it was there until it shattered, and then for years to come you're picking up the pieces—down to the last glassy splinter."

Funerals and obituaries document that a life has ended, but for the survivors, time alone completes that life, and the more it has blended with and flowed alongside our own the more time we need. Two years ago, my brother Frank, a writer, died of complications from diabetes at sixty-three. I don't yet think of him as at rest; his life remains unfinished in me like a draft of a life left behind with a note asking me to revise it and make it cohere. Things keep coming up that I need to discuss with him: J.D. Salinger's death; an article by a professional baseball player describing with lyrical precision how it feels to track a pop fly. Frank adored such topics, and for me, part of thinking about them is still thinking about talking to him about them.

In my father's last year, when he was blind and succumbing to cancer, I mentioned to him a review of a new book by Jimmy Carter entitled, *The Virtues of Aging*. "There are none," he muttered. He would have thought Frank fortunate to be spared the debility of old age, but I still wish my brother had been granted his remaining years. Though Frank's span was nearly complete when he died, my worldly middle school students are proof of how much life can be fit into the decade or so the actuaries say he had coming to him. I never used to think of time as a gift or of myself as a carpe diem kind of guy, but today, thanks to my preoccupation with mortality, I do and I am.

ABOUT THE AUTHORS

Arfah Daud

Arfah Daud was born in Malaysia, but has made her home in the United States for many years now. Daud returns to Malaysia each summer to visit family. A teacher, Daud resides in Monrovia, California. She received her MFA from Antioch University in Los Angeles. Daud's work has appeared in *Susan B and Me*, *Byzantium*, the *Mom Egg*, *Spillway* and *Sin Fronteras*.

Nickie Albert

Nickie Albert is a poet and playwright. Her poems have appeared or are forthcoming in *Wild Goose Review*, *The Legendary*, *Burning Word* and *Ginosko Literary Journal*. She is at work on a new play, "Use No Hooks." She supplements her literary career doing software development and lives in Brooklyn, NY.

Melissa Barrett

Melissa Barrett is the author of *False Soup*, a veg-friendly cookbook from Forklift, Ink. Her poems have received honors from *Narrative*, *Indiana Review*, *Tin House*, *Boxcar Poetry Review*, and *Gulf Coast*, and can be found in recent issues of *Front Porch*, *The Yalobusha Review*, *Storyscape*, and *H_NGM_N*. "Pilot," her collaboration with filmmaker Pete Burkeet, debuted at Video Dumbo. She teaches reading and writing at the high-performing charter school, Columbus Collegiate Academy.

Sophia Boettcher

Sophia Boettcher is an Honors Computer Science major in her third year at college. She recently studied abroad at East China Normal University (ECNU), and helps instruct ESL classes at Lake Washington Institute of Technology in Seattle, Washington. In her leisure time, Sophia enjoys tea, chocolate, coding, writing (science fiction and poetry) and travelling. She hopes to be a part of a high tech start-up company after graduation.

Mark A. Bowers

Mark A. Bowers is a graduate student at Saint Louis University who writes in his ever dwindling and increasingly illusive spare time. He has been published by *The Dallas Review*, *Plain Spoke*, *The Dirty Napkin*, *Carte Blanche*, *The Broken Plate* and *SLAB*. He currently resides in Southwest Missouri where his dazzling wife and their two flawless children graciously put up with him.

Diana Campos

Diana Campos is a 22-year-old Texas native. She is currently majoring in English and plans to continue her education at Texas State University in the fall of 2012. Diana has had two short stories previously published in both her high school's, and college's literary magazines. In her spare time Diana enjoys reading: *The Walking Dead*, *Alice in Wonderland*, and *Harry Potter*.

Joey Connelly

Joey Connelly received his MFA from Ashland University in 2010 and serves as Assistant Professor of English at Kentucky Wesleyan College. His work has appeared or is forthcoming in the *Louisville Review*, *Splinter Generation*, *Medulla Review*, and *New Plains Review*.

Lee Matthew Goldberg

Lee Matthew Goldberg graduated with an MFA from the New School. His fiction has appeared in *Essays & Fictions*, *The Adirondack Review*, *Orion Headless*, *Verdad Magazine*, and *BlazeVOX*. He hosts a monthly reading series called The Guerrilla Lit Fiction Series (guerrillalit. wordpress.com). His articles and reviews have also appeared on fictionwritersreview.com. He's currently working on an adult novel, a short story collection, and a Young Adult trilogy.

Roger A. Hanson, Ph.D.

Dr. Roger A. Hanson is a nascent short story writer

in addition to his role as a legal research and legal reform consultant. His essay *In and about Kabul* shall appear in *Trans-Portal* in January, 2012. His degree in political science is from the University of Minnesota.

Amorak Huey

Amorak Huey left the newspaper business in 2008 after 15 years as a reporter and editor. He teaches writing at Grand Valley State University in Michigan, and his poems have appeared in *The Southern Review*, *Poet Lore*, *Rattle*, *Indiana Review*, *Oxford American*, and other journals.

Kenneth L. Levine

Kenneth L. Levine is a tax attorney who has recently begun to venture into the world of publication, submitting his numerous short stories to an array of journals while also working diligently on creating a novel. Mr. Levine lives in Newington, Connecticut with his girlfriend, two Chihuahuas, and a laptop.

Timothy L. Marsh

Timothy L. Marsh's stories and essays have appeared or are forthcoming in *Quiddity*, *The Evansville Review*, *The Los Angeles Review* and *The New Quarterly*, and are indexed at timothylmarsh. wordpress.com. Recent honors include residency fellowships from the Tenot Foundation-CAMAC Centre d'Arts, and the Montana Artists Refuge to name a few.

Michael Milburn

Michael Milburn teaches high school English in New Haven, Connecticut. His writings have appeared most recently in *New England Review* as well as *Ploughshares*. His third book of poems, *Carpe Something*, is forthcoming in the summer of 2012.

Caroline Misner

Caroline Misner was born in a country that at the time was known as Czechoslovakia. She immigrated to Canada in the summer of 1969.

She is a Pushcart Prize and Journey Prize nominee with numerous published pieces under her belt. Currently, she divides her time between Haliburton and Georgetown, Ontario where she continues to read, write and follow her muse, wherever it may take her.

Aw-o-tan Nisgah
Aw-O-Tan Nisgah is an "adopted" member of the Many Faces People, a family following the Black-feet tradition in Caddo Mills, Texas. His poetry has appeared most recently in *The 2River View*, and—under his birth name—in *Willows Wept Review*, *Barnwood*, and *3:AM Magazine*. He is married to the poet Angela Marie Kaiser. Way-ha!

David Riddle
David Riddle is a student at Fayetteville State University, studying to become an English teacher as a second career. His poems have been published in *Calliope*, *Red Clay Review*, *The Body Attacks Itself*, *Short, Fast and Deadly*, and *The Lyricist*. He has forthcoming publications in *War, Literature & the Arts: An International Journal of the Humanities* and *Chaffey Review*. He writes and raises two young sons in Sanford, North Carolina.

Daniel Saunders
Daniel Saunders is a 24 year old English Education major at the University of Central Oklahoma. He has a beautiful wife, some insane family members, and two hilarious dogs that provide plenty of writing fodder. He enjoys writing fiction, poetry, and comedic non-fiction.

Rob Schultz
Rob Schultz taught American literature at Western Michigan University and Virginia Commonwealth University before drifting into radio and voice work. He published his first novel, *Styll in Love* (Van Neste Books) in 1998, which is still in circulation. Other work has appeared in *Euphony*, *Prime Mincer*, *Rattapallax*, *Slant*, *Sou'wester*, *The MacGuffin* and *West Branch*, among others.

Peter Serchuk

Peter Serchuk's poems have appeared in a variety of journals big and small, among them *Boulevard*, *Denver Quarterly*, *North American Review*, *Valparaiso Poetry Review* and, most recently, *Bayou*, *Naugatuck River Review* and *OVS*. He is the author of two poetry collections: *Waiting for Poppa at the Smithtown Diner* (University of Illinois Press) and *All That Remains*, which will appear in 2012 from WordTech. He lives in Los Angeles.

Andrew Spencer

Andrew Spencer was born in Denver, CO, but currently divides his time between writing and chasing chickens on an organic farm in Yamhill, OR. In addition to writing poetry, Andrew has co-authored a book scheduled for publication in the spring of 2012 by 23 House Publishers titled "Murder in Jefferson: The 1868 Stockade Case," which recounts the true story of a racially charged shoot-out and murder trial in Reconstruction Texas.

Loren Stephens

Loren Stephens is the founder and president of Write Wisdom and Provenance Press, helping clients write and publish their memoirs. She is an award winning documentary filmmaker whose credits include *Legacy of the Hollywood Blacklist*, and the bilingual film, *Los Pastores: The Shepherd's Play*. Her essays and short stories have been published or are forthcoming in *MacGuffin*, *Oracle*, *The Write Room*, and many others.

Thea Swanson

Thea Swanson holds an MFA in fiction from Pacific University, Oregon. She has lived in both poverty and prosperity, at seminary and The Village. She has since moved to Washington where she is amongst tall trees and tall family, taking a position as an English teacher at a local college. More of her stories can be found in such journals as: *Anemone Sidecar*, *Camera Obscura*, *Crab Creek Review*, *Image* and *Our Stories*.

Jacqueline Vogtman

Jacqueline Vogtman's fiction has appeared in *Avery Anthology*, *Berkeley Fiction Review*, *Copper Nickel*, *Drunken Boat*, *Versal*, and other journals. She received her MFA from Bowling Green State University, where she served as an assistant editor of *Mid-American Review*. She lives with her husband and her dog in Northwest New Jersey, where she is currently working on her novel.

Cindy Warren

Cindy Warren has lived in Arizona for over thirty years and graduated from Arizona State University with an Elementary Education degree. She is currently taking a break from teaching kindergarten to write, study, and apply to MFA programs. She is enrolled in fiction and creative non-fiction classes at ASU. "Walking with Buddha" is her first published essay.

James Welsh

James Welsh, originally from Delaware, is now attending graduate school in New York City. Majoring in English literature, James is hoping to teach as a professor one day. He started writing when he was seven years old, and today is rarely seen without a piece of paper and a pen.

Rachel Yu

Rachel is a current student at Stanford Law School. In between highlighting massive textbooks, she runs the foothills around campus and writes it all down.

Shelby Baity – *LeAnne Howe*
Shelby Baity is a junior (Allied Health) at the University of Central Oklahoma.

Randell Baze – *Jim Barnes*
Randell Baze is a senior (Humanities) at the University of Central Oklahoma.

Terri Black – *Robert Conley*
Terri Black is a senior (English Education) at the University of Central Oklahoma.

Rachel Brooks – *Amanda Cobb-Greetham*
Rachel Brooks is a senior (Creative Writing) at the University of Central Oklahoma.

Courtney Cox – *Diane Glancy*
Courtney Cox is a senior (Biology) at the University of Central Oklahoma.

Kelsey Evans – *Judith Houston-Emerson*
Kelsey Evans is a senior (Elementary Education) at the University of Central Oklahoma.

Andrea Gerszewski – *Santee Frazier*
Andrea Gerszewski is a junior (Nursing) at the University of Central Oklahoma.

Brittany Gordon – *Carter Revard*
Brittany Gordon is a senior (English) at the University of Central Oklahoma.

Jesse Haney – *Stuart "Sy" Hoahwah*
Jesse Haney is a senior (Allied Health) at the University of Central Oklahoma.

Shannon Harjo – *Craig Womack*
Shannon Harjo is a senior (Biology) at the University of Central Oklahoma.

Iain Hunter – *Eddie Chuculate*
Iain Hunter is a junior (American Studies) at Swansea University. He is completing coursework at the University of Central Oklahoma during the 2011-12 year.

Ashley Ingalsbe – *Mary Jo Watson*
Ashley Ingalsbe is a junior (English Education) at the University of Central Oklahoma.

Emma Jessee – *Michael Sheyahshe*
Emma Jesse is a senior (English Education) at the University of Central Oklahoma.

Gema Kartomo – *Daniel H. Wilson*
Gema Kartomo is a senior (Biology) at the University of Central Oklahoma.

Amanda Lamb – *Robert Warrior*
Amanda Lamb is a senior (Biology) at the University of Central Oklahoma.

Jessye Patterson – *Les Hannah*
Jessye Patterson is a sophomore (Early Childhood Education) at the University of Central Oklahoma.

Trashon Pelton – *Linda Hogan*
Trashon Pelton is a senior (Dental Hygiene) at the University of Central Oklahoma.

Emily Robnett – *Tim Tingle*
Emily Robnett is a senior (English Education) at the University of Central Oklahoma.

Amanda Sartain – *William Sanders*
Amanda Sartain is a senior (English) at the University of Central Oklahoma.

Jasmine Smith – *N. Scott Momaday*
Jasmine Smith is a junior (English Education) at the University of Central Oklahoma.

Natalie Wessler – *Kimberly Roppolo*
Natalie Wessler is a senior (English Education) at the University of Central Oklahoma.

Kasey Weston – *Sara Sue Hoklotubbe*
Kasey Weston is a senior (Elementary Education) at the University of Central Oklahoma.

Deborah Wood – *Susan Supernaw*
Deborah Wood is a junior (English Education) at the University of Central Oklahoma.

Caroline Wright - *Joy Harjo*

Caroline Wright is a junior (American Studies) at Swansea University. She is completing coursework at the University of Central Oklahoma during the 2011-12 year.

Nai Yang - *Virginia Stroud*

Nai Yang is a senior (Elementary Education) at the University of Central Oklahoma.

www.ingramcontent.com/pod-product-compliance
Lightning Source LLC
Chambersburg PA
CBHW060740180626
46819CB00001B/55